'In *Rethinking Retirement*, Dr De
to reimagine retirement. To unc
tial of the often-dreaded transitio
explores the power of transitions,
within, and takes the reader on
create a meaningful life after work.'

CW00506873

Barbara Waxman, *Odyssey Group
Coaching LLC, TED Speaker*

'Dr Denise Taylor provides you a roadmap along an unex-
plored path from relationships to health, self and wealth
that allows you to be open to discover meaning in the process of re-imagining retirement.'

Kerry Hannon, *workplace futurist,
Yahoo Finance senior columnist and bestselling
author of* In Control at 50+:
How to succeed in the New World of Work

'This practical and inspirational book couldn't be more
timely. With the changes we have seen in recent times to
pensions, health and the world of work, we urgently need
to set outdated assumptions of what retirement should be
aside if we are to truly make the most of twenty-first century life expectancies.'

Catherine Foot,
*Director of Longevity Think Tank,
Phoenix Insights*

'Dr Denise Taylor has written an outstanding blueprint
with practical ideas to help you navigate your journey in
later life. A personal roadmap designed for you.'

Lynda Smith, *Longevity Advocate,
South Africa*

RETHINKING RETIREMENT FOR POSITIVE AGEING

Rethinking Retirement for Positive Ageing is a practical guide that shows you how to make retirement successful, based on the most up-to-date research available. It encourages a deeper and wider view of retirement and reveals how retirement can be a time of transition, renewal, and re-imagination.

Written by career coach Dr Denise Taylor, it considers the psychological factors that impact a successful adjustment to retirement and offers a deeper analysis of how people can find meaning and purpose after full-time work. It examines retirement as an event that often brings about great changes in a person's personal and social life, and how to move forward with meaning in life. Illustrated with interviews, activities, and case studies, and with exercises and questions for reflection, it covers key topics including identity, health, well-being, finances, and relationships.

This insightful guidebook is for all prospective and current retirees as well as employers, careers professionals, and counsellors who want to help people reflect on their approaches to retirement.

Denise Taylor started a series of changes and transitions at age 60 which began with regaining her own identity by becoming single after 39 years of marriage. She completed a Vision Quest 18 months later, a ten-day rite of passage in nature including four days and nights on a 'solo' with no tent and no food. This led to her interest in transitions, particularly the later life transition around retirement. Dr Taylor returned to study, 30 years after gaining an MSc in Occupational Psychology, and at 64, has gained her doctorate and built on her reputation as an expert in helping people find work after 50. Her research has given her expert standing in how to have a successful retirement.

RETHINKING RETIREMENT FOR POSITIVE AGEING

CREATING A MEANINGFUL LIFE AFTER FULL-TIME WORK

Denise Taylor

Routledge
Taylor & Francis Group

LONDON AND NEW YORK

Designed cover image: © Getty Images

First published 2024
by Routledge
4 Park Square, Milton Park, Abingdon, Oxon OX14 4RN

and by Routledge
605 Third Avenue, New York, NY 10158

Routledge is an imprint of the Taylor & Francis Group, an informa business

© 2024 Denise Taylor

The right of Denise Taylor to be identified as author of this work has been asserted in accordance with sections 77 and 78 of the Copyright, Designs and Patents Act 1988.

British Library Cataloguing-in-Publication Data
A catalogue record for this book is available from the British Library

Library of Congress Cataloging-in-Publication Data
Names: Taylor, Denise, 1957 August 29- author.
Title: Rethinking retirement for positive ageing: creating a meaningful life after full-time work / Denise Taylor.
Description: Abingdon, Oxon; New York, NY: Routledge, 2023. | Includes bibliographical references and index.
Identifiers: LCCN 2023021328 (print) | LCCN 2023021329 (ebook) | ISBN 9781032448459 (hardback) | ISBN 9781032448473 (paperback) | ISBN 9781003374206 (ebook)
Subjects: LCSH: Retirement—Social aspects. | Retirement—Psychological aspects. | Retirees—Conduct of life.
Classification: LCC HQ1062 .T38 2023 (print) | LCC HQ1062 (ebook) | DDC 306.3/8—dc23/eng/20230630
LC record available at https://lccn.loc.gov/2023021328
LC ebook record available at https://lccn.loc.gov/2023021329

ISBN: 9781032448459 (hbk)
ISBN: 9781032448473 (pbk)
ISBN: 9781003374206 (ebk)

DOI: 10.4324/9781003374206

Typeset in Optima
by Deanta Global Publishing Services, Chennai

Access the companion website: https://denisetaylor.co.uk/rethinking-retirement/

For my mum Valerie, 90 years young and now a wise elder.

In memory of my dad, Douglas – he loved life till the end.

CONTENTS

Part 3
Renew: Finding meaning and the new you in retirement   **141**

FOREWORD

When you work in the field of career transition you realise that a huge amount of attention is given to work. Work
consumes as well as provides; it takes up most of our best
energy and attention (so it's vitally important to think about
the kind of work we do). We think a great deal about the
presence of work in our lives, so we also think about its
absence – the possibility that work might not be available or
that it might end. Even busy, successful people sometimes
admit worrying about a time when they might be underem-
ployed, or not working.

If people are haunted by the idea that work will end, it's perhaps no surprise that many feel retirement has been thrust upon
them rather than it being a positive choice. Even more see it as
an either/or state of existence.

Building on extensive research and interviews, Dr Taylor
rehearses the fact that traditional retirement planning is focused
on financial and health management issues, and what gives
people meaning in life is ignored.

As we learn what to do with the two, three, or four extra decades of life that we might experience beyond a conventional
career, we're invited by this book to think rather more creatively about pre-retirement and retirement. We can think more
about *redirection* – taking control of circumstances, relishing
change, and experimenting with new experiences.

It's all about learning that work doesn't have to have an on/
off switch but can be part of a personal mixing desk where we

blend different experiences, paid and unpaid, serious and friv-olous. Approached creatively, the years ahead can be a time of real fulfilment.

John Lees
Author of *How to Get a Job You Love*

INTRODUCTION

Why you should read this chapter

This chapter provides some historical context and lets you know what's coming up in the forthcoming chapters. It recognises the recent changes in both retirement and our longer life. We are the young-olds, mainly still fit and healthy until our mid-70s and likely beyond! We want to work on our terms and most importantly we want to live, because we never know how long we have. It recognises the uncertainty of life and how we can be proactive. It also suggests choosing a reflections buddy and keeping a journal to reflect on the work we will do in forthcoming chapters.

This is not the retirement of your parents' generation. No longer is retirement seen as the passage to old age where we can put our feet up and live a life of leisure. On its way out is the four-stage model of childhood, education, work and family, and retirement. Instead, we can move between stages and return to learning, set up a side hustle, or engage in so many options beyond a conventional retirement.

Until the early part of the 20th century there was no retirement – once you could no longer work you were (hopefully) looked after by family. Retirement was introduced around 1930 to make space for younger workers by providing some financial support for persons leaving the workforce. With relatively low life-expectancy rates when retirement benefits were first introduced, most people never lived to fully claim them. With hard

DOI: 10.4324/9781003374206-1

physical work, people were ready to take things easy. The 1970s to the 1990s was the golden era of retirement, with many company pension funds awash with money, people living longer than in the 1930s, and many retiring with a substantial pension and money available to spend on pleasurable activities.

The world is changing and what we thought of as retirement is in flux. There has been a shift from a traditional retirement with a focus on leisure to many different forms of retirement. Will a typical retirement still suit, or, given we still feel fit and healthy, and extra money would be useful, should we carry on working and put traditional ideas of retirement to one side for now?

With many people now living to 90 and beyond, we want more. I've written this book for you if you see the decades ahead full of adventure and growth, so let me help guide you in how to have a fulfilling life after full-time work. I also recognise that some people may feel a bit uncertain about the decades ahead, and so this book will suggest the range of possibilities available to you.

You could be in your 50s and planning ahead or in your 60s and looking forward to this next stage of life. Or perhaps you have already retired and realise you are drifting.

Whilst the money side is important – will I have enough? Where should I invest? Should I opt for an annuity or drawdown as required from my pension pot? The non-financial aspects are equally important. We need to have the psychological resources to move to a later life of meaning where we can remain active and engaged, with curiosity. I want to help you to take stock of your life and look at your options for the future.

If we look at a dictionary definition of retirement it talks about withdrawal; in battle, withdrawal is to fall back or retreat, but we don't want to withdraw, we want to move forward! So perhaps revivement could be a replacement word. When we revive something, we activate, set in motion, renew. We restore things to life. Many people have been sleep-walking through their 50s, on autopilot, not fully satisfied, but not knowing what else there is. So now is the time when we can review – our interests, our relationships, our passions, all those things that make us the person we are.

After taking a broader look at transitions and the process of retirement in Chapter 2, you will get clear on where you are now and consider some thoughts for the future in Chapter 3. We can lose our identity with retirement and many of us have spent too long fitting into what others want, so we will look deeper at this in Chapter 4 where I will help you gain a deeper understanding of the person you are now and what will help you most at this important time of life to continue the journey forward.

You may want to continue to work at your job as long as possible. This may be because you need the money, or you may love your job and want to continue for as long as it is satisfying. Perhaps your work has been your life and you aren't sure what else you could do, so you will just carry on. Unfortunately, some people who continue to work realise too late that they have wasted this wonderful period of life. I don't want you to be one of them. We will consider what work means to you in Chapter 5. Travel could be your goal – you want to see more of the world. Or maybe it's around rekindling interests in a hobby. You've got the guitar out of the loft, and your partner is considering painting. Perhaps you both wonder if you could make some money through turning a hobby into a small business. This is a part of filling the gap of the time we previously spent working and is also covered in this chapter.

At our age, we have many things going in our favour, but there are also likely some obstacles to overcome. You may have some health issues, or a big life change as your partner has decided they want to move on, and you never saw it coming, or perhaps you are experiencing sadness with the death of someone close to you. This could be a time when you are still financially responsible for your children and/or you also have the task of caring for your elderly relatives. All these things take time, money, and our energy, so we need to look after ourselves too. We will look at relationships – the one with ourselves, with our partners, with our wider family, with our friends, and with our role in society. I cover health in Chapter 6, relationships in Chapter 7, and money in Chapter 8.

In this book we will look at your options and help you to create a life ahead that's right for you. And we will go deeper into having a meaningful life in Part 3.

I've written this book so you can dip in and out. Choose what seems relevant to you and read and follow the activities so you can draw up a blueprint to suit the person you are now. But don't forget that the choices you make now are not forever – you can make changes at any time.

This book will help you to pause, to reflect and to move forward with intention.

You have many options and I want to be your guide so that at, perhaps age 80, you can look back and be content with the decisions made now.

I've included a number of activities to get you thinking and you may want to get a journal to capture your notes. It could be helpful to have a 'reflections buddy' too.

Reflections buddy and journalling

Whilst you can work on all the activities in this book alone, it makes a good deal of sense to work along with someone else so you can talk out loud and get a different perspective to your own. You may choose the same person throughout, or at times a different person may feel more appropriate. For me, I would choose someone who I would feel safe disclosing personal information with and who would be interested in my dreams and ideas. They would gently motivate me, and would listen and encourage me to talk further. Or you may be someone who may need more encouraging and to have someone who is there to hold you to account.

You can also write things down in a notebook or journal. It can be cathartic to open up in some areas, knowing that you are the only person who will ever read it. I find writing in a notebook is a very different experience than typing words into a document. It's the movement of pen on paper that can encourage deeper reflections.

Through working with others and using your journal you will be taking an active role in your plans for the time ahead. Find a nice pen and notebook – maybe go and buy new ones – and consider who you would like to ask to be your reflections buddy.

WHAT IS RETIREMENT?

A good question – even researchers can't agree on a definition[1] and it's no longer defined by reaching a specific chronological age.[2] The retirement age is increasing, and people are living longer, although not necessarily in good health.[3] There is no longer a fixed retirement date, pensions are moving from defined benefits to defined contribution, and there is less certainty over pension levels. However, at some point, most people will disengage from full-time work, and classify themselves as retired.

Retirement has been defined in various ways by different researchers, based on the research questions being addressed and the researcher's disciplinary background.[4] Generally, it covers an individual leaving the work force with a drop in their commitment to work.[5] It's a major transition in older workers' lives[6] and is a social phenomenon that is changing. What we understand by retirement has significantly changed over the last 50 years.[7] In the 1950s, there would have been a shared agreement over what this word meant. Back then it was assumed people would exit the workforce, aged 65 for men, and 60 for women, with limited options.[8] We now have many more choices that we can consider. Retirement can be voluntary, which is generally chosen when people have economic security via pension and savings,[9] or involuntary due to reorganisation or health reasons.[10]

There is now diversity in people's experience and the options they might choose. Some will choose a 'clean break' and stop work entirely. Others will take a phased approach, continuing with part-time work for a period of time. For some, retirement will become temporary with the options of 'unretirement', where people return to work after retirement, either full- or part-time,[11] or enter into 'encore careers' where people take on a new 'person-driven job' with a focus on meaning and social impact.[12]

Retirement can thus be seen as a number of transitions as we move into different phases, try out different options, and choose the balance of paid and non-paid activity that suits the person we are now. As we age, we will often seek to focus more on activity that contributes to the well-being of society. Retirement has often been thought of as 'what it is not' – a state of not working,[13] but today you can think of yourself as retired and still undertake some paid work. In Korea, retirement means 'to retire from one's primary work rather than retire entirely from work'.[14] From our Western perspective we see retirement as a time of freedom, individuality, and independence, but this is not the view from all cultures.

One of the problems with a definition of retirement is that the 'post full-time work' period can cover a very broad time span. Given that retirement can last for more than 30 years, retirement should perhaps be divided into different periods with accompanying transitions similar to childhood.[15] We are different at 60 to 80, and we all know 80-year-olds, even 90-year-olds, full of *joie de vivre* and 50-year-olds who act old and see themselves as past it. So, consider this: should the early part of retirement be given a new name? Adolescence was only introduced in 1904 – there was no name for this life stage before then. I like the term 'y-olds' (the young- olds).

The young-olds (yolds)

The y-olds sound like a pop group, and it's a term I frequently used during both my academic research and writing this book. In fact, I consider myself one of them! We are the people between the conventional end of working age and old age. We are in relatively good health, we want to work on our terms, and, most importantly, we want to live, because we never know how long we have. There is so much to do, and it's not just for ourselves but how we can offer more to the wider world. We want to feel that we matter. Part 3 will get us thinking about this.

What's useful to consider is that whilst retirement is predictable, individuals experience it in different ways. Retirement is an event that often brings about great changes in a person's personal and social life. For many people, work was not only a way to fill time and earn money, but also important for their identity and meaning in life. After retirement, these benefits of work are lost. We lose status derived from the job, and there is also the loss of the meaning and purpose that we had gained from our work. We need to fill this with something else that gives us meaning, and that will differ between people. What is meaningful to me may not be relevant to you, and vice versa.

For some, retirement is seen as a negative. Some may be focused on regret and loss, yet others see it as a time of growth and development, involving new activities, such as joining clubs, attending the theatre and sporting events.[16] Some see retirement as a sign of success; they have achieved their long-term goal, and this can lead to greater life satisfaction. Yet others focus more on their loss of status which was associated with their work identity.[17] There are personal characteristics that help us remain motivated and able to adapt in a positive way[18] and this will be covered in Chapter 4, where we look at psychological factors.

You've undoubtedly gathered that my focus is much more on life ahead, rather than the regrets that come from the past; simply put, you are not too old, and it is not too late. There are so many possibilities ahead of us. For a mountaineer, reaching the summit is not the ultimate goal – you also need to get back down. Leaving our full-time job is not the end of our productive life, but a time to move on to other goals and plans.

What would you love to do? You may have 20+ years ahead, or it could be 40 years. Consider that there is likely plenty of time to learn something, do something … focus on something that interests you, that you are passionate about and that you can do. I like the term 're-tyre', instead of 'retire' – a time to change tyres (I know my American readers spell tyre as tire, so assume the English spelling!) and move forward with intention. Have you ever thought of this?

PREPARATION FOR RETIREMENT

I've been involved in leading pre-retirement seminars since the mid-1980s and the main topic was financial matters, followed by health. We did include discussions on hobbies and interests but there was not much discussion on how we will change as individuals and what gives us meaning. So much of the media aimed at people of our age is focused on spending money and taking things easy, but ask yourself this: do you really want a life of *only* leisure and pleasure following retirement?

We are living longer, we've gained an extra 30 to 40 years on average over the past 100 years, so we have the opportunity to create a fulfilled life in our later years. Some will want to get more meaning into their life, but they have few role models. This book will encourage you to take a deeper and wider view than what is usually covered in retirement preparation courses, and meaning is specifically covered in Part 3.

However, while we may be living longer on average, this may not necessarily be in good health, and we never know if we will have a health setback. What to consider in connection with health and well-being will be covered in Chapter 6. Writing this in 2023, it is clear that we have less certainty in life. With pensions moving from defined benefits to defined contribution, we can worry if we will have enough money for a comfortable retirement. Our financial situation is important and will be addressed in Chapter 8.

Whilst adequate finances and good health are important factors for retirement, these are not easy to improve once you are close to retirement. We are going to look at both areas in the coming chapters. What can help, whatever our other circumstances, are certain psychological factors, such as values, locus of control, self-efficacy, and mastery and I talk about this in Chapter 4 and, like the people I work with, I know you will find some fascinating insights here.

A SUCCESSFUL RETIREMENT

Let's get this out in the open straight away: all the research says that for a successful adjustment to retirement, we need to have good physical health, adequate finances, strong psychological health, and a sense of meaning gained through leisure, voluntary activity, and social integration.[19] But what if we don't? A small pension can be supplemented with paid work; in poor health we can make adjustments; we can seek to become more resilient; and we can look for other ways to improve life.

Our psychological health is influenced by (1) our physical health, and how we come to terms with health changes, (2) pre-retirement job-related factors (e.g., work stress), (3) family-related factors such as our marital status, (4) retirement transition-related factors (e.g., retirement planning), and also (5) post-retirement activities such as bridge employment and leisure activities.[20] So, everything in this book inter-relates.

I've included some self-assessments coming up in Chapter 3 so you can see how you score in a wide variety of areas. I've included them so you can take some initial measurements of yourself and expect that these assessments will help you decide where to focus.

THE RESEARCH

As a psychologist, aged 65 as I wrote this book, what has fascinated me is how an understanding of our own psychology, including personality, can make such a difference to how we move into retirement, including helping us to live longer. Looking deep into this, it was astounding to find these matters hadn't been covered in any depth and the available research I found was seen as inconsistent.[21] Most research was focused on a review of income, health, age, marital status, and conditions for exiting the workplace as predicting successful retirement adjustment. I had found a gap, and set out to look at the psychological factors. There was me, in my 60s, researching on what will make a difference to people like us.

My research began with a systematic review (where research is conducted into all studies based on a specific term, or, in my case, terms). I reviewed studies undertaken in the USA, Australia, Canada, Sweden, France, Netherlands, Nigeria, Spain, and the UK and involved a total population of almost 11,000 people with mainly a balanced split between the sexes. Individuals were aged 58 to 71 and had taken retirement at least 12 months before the research and up to nine years after. I then undertook in-depth interviews where I fully immersed myself in understanding a smaller number of people.

All the people I include in this book are either clients I worked with or people I talked to as part of my research.

This introduction is to get you ready for what lies ahead in this book. I may be now seen by some as an academic but this is not a stuffy textbook. It's intended to be a practical guide we can work through to help you have the retirement that is right for you and to set in motion the action and activities to achieve this.

I'm excited to be on this journey with you.

ONE LAST THING BEFORE YOU MOVE ON ...

I'd like you to write a note to yourself, in the form of a letter, perhaps on what you are hoping to get from this book and retirement. Ask yourself this question: What does a successful retirement look like to you?

NOTES

1 Shultz, K.S., & Wang, M. (2011). Psychological perspectives on the changing nature of retirement. *American Psychologist*, 66,170–179.

2 Moen, P., Kim, J.E., & Hofmeister, H. (2001). Couples' work/retirement transitions, gender, and marital quality. *Social Psychology Quarterly*, 64, 55–71.

3 Brown, G.C. (2015). Living too long, *EMBO Report*, Feb; 16(2), 137–141.

4 Denton, F.T., & Spencer, B.G. (2009). What is retirement? A review and assessment of alternative concepts and measures. *Canadian Journal on Aging / La Revue canadienne du vieillissement*, 28(1), 63–76.

5 Shultz & Wang, Psychological perspectives on the changing nature of retirement.

6 Kubicek, B., Korunka, C., Raymo, J.M., & Hoonakker, P. (2011). Psychological well-being in retirement: The effects of personal and gendered contextual resources. *Journal of Occupational Health Psychology*, 16(2), 230–246.

7 Shultz, K., Shultz, K.S., & Henkens, K. (2010). Introduction to the changing nature of retirement: an international perspective. *International Journal of Manpower*, 31(3), 265–270.

8 Moen, P. (2003). Midcourse. In: Mortimer J.T. & Shanahan M.J. (eds), *Handbook of the Life Course. Handbooks of Sociology and Social Research*. Springer, Boston, MA.

9 Nilsson, K., Hydbom, A.R., & Rylander, L. (2011). Factors influencing the decision to extend working life or retire. *Scandinavian Journal of Work, Environment & Health*, 37, 473–480.

10 Schultz, K.S., Morton, K.R., & Weckerle, J.R. (1998). The influence of push and pull factors on voluntary and involuntary early retirees' retirement decision and adjustment. *Journal of Vocational Behavior.* 53, 45–57.

11 Maestas, N. (2010). Back to work: Expectations and realizations of work after retirement. *Journal of Human Resources, 45*(3), 718–748.

12 Freedman, M. (2007). *Encore: Finding work that matters in the second half of life.* Cambridge, MA: Perseus, Fredrickson.

13 Denton & Spencer, What is retirement?

14 Kim, S.J. (2014). The career transition process: A qualitative exploration of korean middle-aged workers in postretirement employment. *Adult Education Quarterly*, 64(1), 3–19.

15 MacBean, E. C. (2007). Retirement realities: Retirement just ain't what it used to be. *Journal of Financial Service Professionals*, 61(1), 40–50.

16 Guerriero-Austrom, M., Perkins, A.J., Damush, T.M., & Hendrie, H.C. (2003). Predictors of life satisfaction in retired physicians and spouses. *Social Psychiatry and Psychiatric Epidemiology*, 38, 134–141.

17 Jones, I.R., Leontowitsch, M., & Higgs, P. (2010). The experience of retirement in second modernity generational habitus among retired senior managers. *Sociology,* 44(1), 103–120.

18 Stephan, Y., Fouquereau, E., & Fernandez, A. (2008). The relation between self-determination and retirement satisfaction among active retired individuals. *The International Journal of Aging and Human Development*, 66(4), 329–345.

19 Barbosa, L.M., Monteiro, B., & Murta, S.G. (2016). Retirement adjustment predictors - A systematic review. *Work, Aging and Retirement*, 2(2), 262–280.

20 Wang, M., & Hesketh, B. (2012). Achieving well-being in retirement: Recommendations from 20 years of research. *SIOP White Paper Series.*

21 Kim, J.E., & Moen, P. (2002). Retirement transitions, gender, and psychological well-being: A life-course, ecological model. *Journals of Gerontology: Psychological Sciences*, 57B, 212–222.

PART 1

REFLECT

Reflecting on your retirement

TRANSITIONS – THE PROCESS OF RETIREMENT

Why you should read this chapter

We go through many transitions in life, and alongside the transition from full-time work we also have the transition to an older stage of life. This chapter discusses how retirement is a process, how life changes after retirement, and takes you through the stages of transition with activities to get you to consider previous transitions in your life. You will learn that transitions are not situational but psychological. It is not meant to be easy; we will have challenges, just like how a butterfly emerges from a cocoon. We need to mark the transition, and whilst this could be via a party or a 'big holiday', we can also create a ritual, and suggestions to do this are included.

Our life has been full of change and transitions: major ones such as starting school and moving to university. The transitions to our first job to marriage/living together and then becoming a parent, and many smaller ones too, such as moving home, change of job, change in health and more.

THE RETIREMENT TRANSITION

As we grow older, our behaviour is determined by transitions, not age. As we grow older, there are more differences between us than similarities. This differs from when we move from infancy through childhood to adolescence, where there are similarities between individuals of the same age. Individuals

DOI: 10.4324/9781003374206-3

can become parents from their late teens until much later in life, for example. It is the transition (marriage, divorce, death of a child, retirement) that brings people together rather than a chronological age.[1]

And now we reach retirement. This is a unique transition in our lives that involves changes in roles, relationships, and daily routines as well as shifts in income and in health. We gain a substantial amount of free time, with increased opportunities for living the good life, such as spending time with friends and family and pursuing satisfying activities. This is a time with greater freedom, where we can avail ourselves of opportunities we didn't have when working,[2] and we can focus on new interests and sources of pleasure.[3] Whilst many think money is the most important factor, personal motivation will have a major impact on how well we, the retirees, adjust to retirement.

Previously seen as a crisis, in which the older worker's physical and mental health was threatened and a single negative event,[4] researchers now view retirement as a process,[5] and the transition from work to retirement can take several years to be concluded,[6] so we shouldn't expect it to be quick and easy. It is a subjective journey involving a psychosocial transition rather than a single event of leaving the workplace and it may be related to psychological well-being.[7] Too many people focus on the money side, unaware that what is happening internally has a major influence on whether we have a successful transition.

There are three broad phases of retirement.[8] **Pre-retirement**, when we are still working and are considering our future; **a transition period**, where there is often initial euphoria, and then some stress as we consider the complexities of choice and begin to consider our adjustments to a new lifestyle. This may last varying lengths of time and involve multiple changes in employment status. Finally, we reach the **adjustment phase**, when we have settled into this life stage and we see ourselves as retired. This adjustment can take time and is a dynamic and ongoing process potentially with multiple alternating periods of stabilisation and readjustment, sometimes affected by external factors. We don't go through any change, including retirement, in a vacuum. [9]

This chapter will talk us through transitions and clarify the steps we need to complete. We will consider many of the blocks and challenges that may come up at some point in the future. It is better to do it now than later in life when change becomes even more challenging. This reminds me of a conversation with my trainer at the gym. I was struggling with using a particular piece of gym equipment and asked him why I can't do the exercises that I can already do! He said I'm doing this specific exercise to give me the strength to reach for things from a high shelf safely, which will be beneficial as I age. Whilst it is hard for me now, he said that it's better for me to persevere to make life easier later, or I can keep to easy things now, and struggle later. Such a helpful way of looking at things, and relevant to us as we age. Let's put in the effort now so we can have a smooth and easier later life.

Change and transitions

Retirement is a major change, but we transition in different ways, and it is in the transitions where we grow. We need to adjust to the loss of our work role and the creation of our new lifestyle. We also need to take time to go through the transition so we can adapt to the new life stage of retirement. Transition can include both external resources (e.g., a phased retirement) and internal resources, especially psychological factors.

An interesting way to look at the difference between change and transition is that a change is where something **situational** has gone on. George was married, got divorced, and remarried. But nothing had changed within; he held the same beliefs and attitudes and the reasons why his marriage ended repeated itself in the next one. **A transition is not situational, but psychological**. After a divorce Cara took time to understand who she was, her part in the breakup, and the person she wanted to be going into the next relationship. She was far more likely to have success, and she did!

With the transition to retirement, some will fear the change and prefer the comfort of what they already know. For some, it is easier to stay working and to put off any decision. Why leave the job that has meant so much in terms of our identity and self-worth and head towards uncertainty when we can post-pone the decision? Surely, we can keep going just a little bit longer – another year, or two, or three.

We know how other people have made the change, but they aren't us. And however much they sing the praises of their choice, how much of that is as justification? They may be experiencing cognitive dissonance, where there is inconsistency in their beliefs and behaviours. When people tell us they were never happier, do they really mean it or are they adjusting how they feel to match what they say.[10]

In the transition phase of retirement there is often excitement over how to fill our days, with time for hobbies, interests, and travels. However, when work has provided people with a meaningful experience, there is a gap to be filled. The experience of retirement can be the trigger for people to seek meaning in their lives and to review and reflect on their life to date, to get a sense of where their life is heading. This can lead some people to make significant changes as they consider life priorities, values, and future goals. We look into this in Part 3.

Individuals need to adjust to the loss of their work role and the creation of a new lifestyle.[11] They need to take time to go through this initial transition so they can gain retirement adjustment and then adapt to the new life stage of retirement.[12] Adjustment to retirement includes how people fit into the wider environment of the outside world.[13]

Moving to a life after full-time work can lead to a loss of status, but people can also potentially lose the meaning and purpose that has been gained from their work. After retirement, people may question if they still have a useful role in society. Many people have status and identity through their work, and careers can be seen around mattering.[14] To what extent do people 'matter' without work? Not everyone wants to take on the identity of 'retired'. We cover mattering in Chapter 9.

We continually experience transitions; currently I have a change of focus in my work (career), resuming weight training (health), illness with two close family members (family) and my partner moving in with me (relationship) before we move into a new home together (house move).

You have to decide what works best for you, to go through one transition at a time or to go all in. Jim is changing jobs (down to redundancy), leaving his long-term relationship, and now having to get his own place to live. Added to this is one child needing his emotional support whilst living overseas, and he has to take care of his health following a heart attack two years before. He never expected to experience so many things at once. Ideally, it would be one thing at a time, but he has had to work out how to manage this series of transitions and remain well. He'd expected a traditional retirement, but the breakup of his relationship has delayed that, so he also has the emotional impact of this loss.

Activity 2.1

Before looking forward to this retirement transition, let's look back at a significant change in your life. It could be work or personal, but something that stands out. Grab your journal or notebook and write down as much as you can remember about how you made a significant transition in your life. You may like to talk about this with your reflections buddy.

Kim wrote about a work change, as there had been a major reorganisation a couple of years before. Her job changed and she had to move location. All of this was happening to her, and the company managed it well. But now, as she considered her future, it was different. She was much more invested in her own future and the decisions would be hers.

Cara remembered the successful transition she completed after the end of a long marriage, to become the person that was lost in a marriage. She recalled the sadness, and setbacks, and then the joy she experienced as she realised that she had found herself. It had taken time, and at times it had been painful, but she recognised how all of this helped her to successfully manage the transition.

Generative and regressive transitions

What you may have noticed is that you have made decisions in one of two ways. We can see transitions as something that happens to us (**regressive**) or something where we are more in control (**generative**). The regressive option allows us to decide fast, as this is the easiest. This is the option Sophie chose. The alternative is to take more time, invest more, and choose a generative change.

Not able to retire till she got her pension at 66, following redundancy, aged 61, Sophie decided to move to a similar job. She knew it wasn't the right job for her but accepted it as it was the easy option. She started coaching sessions with me when, a year later, she realised she had played it too safe. In other situations, people can stay in an unhappy marriage because they are afraid of being judged by friends and family, or society/church/community. These are regressive transitions.

The generative option was chosen by Paul. He faced a choice of what to do aged 63. He could retire and give up work completely, but he wanted to spend time working out what was going to give him the most meaningful life ahead and he certainly didn't want to feel like he was wasting his time. We worked together over a number of months to enable him to fully work through alternatives. When people take time to work through a change, they are using a regenerative process, which reminds us of when a caterpillar becomes a butterfly. From the outside, nothing appears to be happening, but inside is completely different and this is where the transformation occurs. This internal change is important.

UNDERSTANDING TRANSITIONS

So many of the people I talk with were knocked sideways by the retirement transition; they mainly hadn't given any thought to the process and got thrown as things didn't work out as planned. I want to talk it through with you now, as it is relevant both to this passage into retirement and also to other changes in your life. In his book, *Life is in the Transitions*, Bruce Feiler writes about how we experience 36 transitions in our adult life alongside life-quakes such as death, divorce, loss of job. Many of them were not initiated by us, such as when we're made redundant, a life-changing accident, finding our partner has cheated on us. There are also those we choose, such as quitting drugs or alcohol, changing religion, starting a new initiative. We all have plenty of experience of transitions, some done well, others less so, and the activity above would have got you thinking on these.

Activity 2.2

Reflect on the transitions you have gone through: what have you noticed about how you personally have handled the transition? What will help you improve the experience for this one, especially on ways of dealing with potential dips and setbacks? Make a note in your journal.

For most older people, retirement is not only a major life transition between middle and late adulthood (65 and older) but is also associated with important psychological and interpersonal changes that may impact on their self-esteem and well-being.[15] This is a transition to the later stages of life and an introduction to the realities of ageing, the start of a decline in health and noticing age-related physical and cognitive changes in themselves and others, alongside the mortality of relatives and friends.[16] Whilst for some the transition is smooth, up to one third of people who retire find the transition either stressful or notice a decline in their well-being.[17] van Solinge[18] reports that between 10 and 25 per cent of older workers experience difficulties in adjusting to retirement and in the UK, 25 per cent of retirees experience difficulties which can affect mental health.[19]

The transition from being a worker to a retired person can be seen as a macro-role identity transition which follows a three-stage model:[20] (1) exit from the present role, (2) a period of transition that can be marked by rites of passage and liminality, and eventually (3) entry into the new role. This is in line with the three-stage rite-of-passage model invented by Van Gennop,[21] which includes the three stages of severance, threshold, and incorporation and is the basis of the transition model created by William Bridges.[22] The model sounds simple, but as retirement is a major transition it can affect people differently and not everyone does things in order. You can have a new beginning and then have to go back to a different stage to complete the ending.

As we go through change, we go through three stages:

1. Endings, losing, and letting go.
2. The neutral zone (liminal space).
3. The new beginning.

1: Endings, losing, and letting go

A transition usually starts with an ending. Even when this is something we have chosen, it can still be unsettling and painful. It's important to be aware of how we feel, and some of the negative feelings that come up for people include anger, denial, disorientation, fear, frustration, guilt, sadness, tired, uncertainty, and a sense of loss. It is too easy to deny our feelings. Patrick had had a health scare and whilst worried over the impact on his future he didn't want to burden his loved one with his fears. Many of the people I work with have a deep sense of uncertainty as to what will be their identity once they leave their job.

Activity 2.3

Take a moment to think about how you are feeling now, both positive and negative, or how you felt once you started to consider retirement. How many of these emotions did you feel. Whilst I've noted the negative ones above, it could perhaps have been excitement, curiosity, and joy. Make a note in your journal.

Endings take time, and there can be false endings as the steps we take haven't worked out; but from this we learn and grow. With retirement, we have a major ending to life as we know it, with the move to something else. We can be in control, to take it at the pace we like, and a move to part-time working can enable us to get used to having more time. We discuss this in Chapter 5.

If we think of other transitions in our lives, we will probably recall how some were externally generated – a redundancy came out of the blue, we were blind-sided to find out that we were cheated on by our partner. Other times they were internally driven. We were the one to end a relationship as we knew things weren't working, and we knew we had to leave our job as it wasn't doing our health any good. And others, even though we knew they were happening, had a greater impact on us than we expected, such as our last child leaving home or the death of an elderly parent.

An end involves letting go, and this can include letting go of our thoughts, feelings, relationships, and expectations. We can think about our work, and how we feel about saying goodbye to colleagues, what we will miss, and also what we will be glad to say goodbye to. Unless we have the ending, there is no space for something new. Whilst moving on into retirement is less of a loss and more of a new beginning, it will still lead to an emotional reaction. It helps to mark the ending in some way.

Too many people drift into retirement and lack the clear transition as found in more Indigenous cultures gained through a 'rite of passage'. In time gone by, there was a retirement party with a gold watch or a clock and a bit of a party; I remember my first boss leaving for the final time, and he looked so sad as he packed his belongings into his car.

Activity 2.4

Have you thought of a way of celebrating this ending as you move into retirement? A party is the obvious one but it could be time on a retreat, or something else. See my ritual for turning 65, below, or the call-out box on creating your own ritual. You may like to start creating your retirement ritual.

Whilst we have more autonomy on when to retire, without something to mark a clear break into a life away from the workplace, people can feel 'unmoored' and lacking guidance on how to manage the transition. This is why I recommend a way of marking the transition point. Whilst I'd opted for 'big holidays' as I turned 50 and 60, I wanted to do something different as I reached 65. I decided to spend a day out in nature. Wild camping overnight, listening to the owls and deer I dropped into the natural environment, all ready to recognise the return of my birth date.

> I woke at dawn, had a hot drink and sat quietly in reflection. My phone was switched off, my watch was in my bag. I smudged with sage. I drummed a little. I danced. I prayed. I spoke to the trees around me. I'd taken some poems to reflect on. Many people I knew had sent me heartfelt messages and quotes. I read and cried. I danced. And I wrote … pages and pages in my journal. I reflected on where I was in my life right now – work, relationships, health. And then I looked back. Right back to my late teens. And then more time on the last five years. I thought about how far I'd come. The changes I'd made. Personal – a new single life and independence. Work – moving towards retirement and transition work. Changes in relationships with family. Undertaking two Vision Quests and now supporting others as a Vision Quest guide. Gaining weight, not losing it but also regaining fitness and accepting my body. Being kinder to myself, and not putting up with things. This is the time to be true to me. With all these changes over the last five years, thinking how awesome life will be moving forward. What changes and achievements will happen between now and 70. I'm excited for my future. Over the hill – nah! I've climbed that hill and looking ahead – I'm nowhere need the end.

Creating a ritual

Creating a ritual around a transition can be a powerful way to mark a significant change in your life; it can be retirement, it could also be a move, or the end of a relationship. Here are some suggestions for creating a meaningful ritual:

Choose a location: select a place that has personal significance to you, such as a favourite park, woodland, beach, or mountain. This will make the ritual more meaningful and help you connect with the transition you're experiencing.

Set an intention: think about what you hope to achieve through this ritual. Is it closure, a sense of release, or a fresh start? Whatever it may be, set an intention.

Create a ritual activity: this could be anything from lighting a candle or writing a letter to yourself to burying a symbolic object or reciting a personal mantra. Choose an activity that feels meaningful to you. You can make it as comprehensive as you want.

Gather support: you may want to invite friends or family members to participate in the ritual with you, or simply let them know what you're doing so they can offer support.

Reflect and celebrate: after completing the ritual, take some time to reflect on the experience and celebrate the transition you've made. Recognise the significance of this moment in your life and feel proud of yourself for taking this step.

2: Neutral zone

After the ending, comes deciding where to go next. Liminal spaces are where we are betwixt and between the familiar and the completely unknown. It's a stage that we need to move through, and it can take time. Chip Conley[23] refers to this as the 'messy middle'. We are letting go of the old and not yet sure of what is to come. I'm reminded of *A Midsummer Night's Dream* where the couples go into the forest and come out and they are changed.

This can be a time where we feel like nothing is happening. If we were a caterpillar, this is the stage when we are in the gooey soup, in our cocoon. As humans, we are in a state of uncertainty; we know we have to let go but we have yet to find our new selves. This can lead to feeling stuck and uncertain but it can also be a time of creativity and openness to the range of possibilities. Being creative can help to free up our thinking; perhaps this is the time to take up dancing, singing, or painting, or to join a comedy class. Long walks with a focus on noticing nature – what we see, the feel of the breeze etc. can give our mind a rest. Taking ourselves away from the situation gives our brain a chance to think and feel what is right for us. The focus is on being in the moment, and at home we could sit quietly, light a scented candle, and sit with silence.

We need to allow time to work out what is right for us, to perhaps try out some options, to think things through, to talk with an external coach, or be open with our family. If we rush this stage, we may not do it well and have to return. We knew what our life was like before; we are now in a period of uncertainty. We may be feeling vulnerable. This is when we need to allow time to explore, to understand who we are, what we want, so we can plan and find the thread that has been with us through our lives. Much in Chapter 4 about personality and self-discovery is going to be of help here. You will want to understand your skills and values and use your curiosity to explore. Whilst there will be uncertainty and fear, taking a growth mindset approach, where you are more open to possibilities and ready to try out new things, will help you to find momentum and take the first step, and then the next one. You recognise that there will be setbacks and will be ready for them.

Transition can be stressful and exciting. How we see it is our choice. There is so much possibility, but many focus on the negative as they want to stay safe. This is the time when some people get scared, they are worried, and backtrack to a place of safety. They hold on to the default and don't let go, staying in this middle phase; perhaps to stay with what they were doing before, but they will need to return to this at a later stage.

It can help to invest in ourselves as we consider our future. We may need to gain specific skills, or we may want to take time to get a deeper understanding of who we are. Some will take a time out, space to allow themselves to grow. Like a plant whose roots have no room to spread. If you repot yourself into new soil, it allows you space to become the person you want to be. Lynda did this by moving to Italy for a year, immersing herself in learning the language and allowing herself time to consider how she wanted her life to be at 65 and moving forward.

She continued with some work, and for her a desk-based jobs for four hours, four days a week suited her perfectly.

In this phase you may like to think of what you need to let go of. This could be possessions you no longer need. Arthur disposed of over a dozen suits and 30 ties when he retired and knew he would never need to wear formal wear again. It could be relationships; why do we spend time with people who take away our energy, or with whom we no longer have common interests. Maybe it is to let go of a dream. You now realise you will never get the house in the country with a couple of acres of land, but what could you get instead?

Time to also think about what you want more of. You may want different people around you, a new loving relationship, to learn something new. We can learn so much from taking a beginners' perspective. Finally, what do you want to hold on to? For me it is about maintaining fitness, so I am as strong at 75 as at 65 and can maintain my level of activities.

You may fear failure, but what if it gets so much better. Ian was holding back on moving forward in his relationship with Susanne, for them to buy a property together in their late 60s. He focused on everything that could go wrong but with couples counselling he changed his perspective to see how life could truly excel if he was fully open to a new life with Susanne. It's useful to think about how to optimise your future, what you can do to improve all aspects of your life.

Activity 2.5

What do you need to let go of? It helps to write things down and to make a plan to let go. What do you want more of and how will you get it. What do you want to hold on to? Are you afraid of anything? It helps to get it out in the open, so write it all down in your journal. You may like to chat about this with your reflections buddy.

That may have taken some time, and it may not be finished. Keep your notes handy so you can review and add to them again. Add in detail so you have a clear plan and not just a vague thought.

3: The new beginning

And we then come through and become the butterfly. Working through the following chapters, we will know who we are, our values and our strengths, and what we want to be. We will be open and looking forward to the new life ahead and to what we will become.

Having a supporter

We can feel alone in a transition, so it's helpful to find someone who can help us. For some, their partner fits the bill. Others will seek an external coach and some prefer to work in a group. Maybe you have some good friends to call on. This could be your reflections buddy or someone else. Whether it be for this retirement transition or another one, you want to consider the type of support you want. Bruce Feiler[24] writes about these different roles. Do you want to have a **'comforter'**. Someone who is on your side and believes in you. Maybe you need a bit more, someone to suggest ideas for you to consider; these are the **'nudgers'**. Maybe you need something more like a boot-camp approach. These are referred to as **'slappers'**, who seek to get you out of your funk and say things like – 'I'm fed up with listening to you, get up and do something!' Or the **'modellers'**, who can be seen as role models offering guidance such as a retirement coach who really understands you. There are also the **'naysayers'** who tell us we can never do whatever it is we are trying to do. Whilst these are not supportive, some people find them motivational, as they seek to prove them wrong. So, if you want support from other people, make clear the type of support you want so neither of you is frustrated.

We need to adjust to the loss of our work role and the creation of a new lifestyle[25] and need to take time to go through the initial transition so we can gain retirement adjustment and then adapt to the new life stage of retirement. For some people the transition will be positive and expected, for others a more negative experience, and people will take varying amounts of time to move through the stages to adjustment. People bring different strengths and experiences to the situation, have differing levels of support and different coping strategies.[26]

Not everyone experiences a smooth transition. This can be down to the loss of challenge and purpose that is associated with one's career. Leaving a challenging job is related to less satisfaction in retirement.[27] Though some retired individuals spend more time doing enjoyable activities compared to full-time employees, for others they have less variety in their daily tasks, do less problem-solving, are less likely to learn new things, and have significantly fewer positive social interactions.[28]

Research suggests that the early retirement experience (six months or less since retirement) may be significantly different than the experience a year after leaving the workforce.[29] That's why I focused on people a year or more beyond retirement. Many of us will remain in the middle transition stage for some time. We can remain attached to our profession, and work centrality (our connection to our work) will be stronger during the first year after retirement, increasing perceptions of losses, but it declines with time[30] as we welcome our new life stage.

We know that adjustment to retirement takes time and depends on whether our work was fulfilling or stressful, alongside our health, finances, and our relationships with others. The process of adjusting to retirement may differ, both across time and between individuals. Retirement adjustment is reached when people have successfully negotiated the retirement transition.[31] Retirement adjustment may not be a 'one time' event and it can affect us over time. It is reached when we have worked through the transition, accept our new life stage, and we feel comfortable with retirement.

Retirement transition

As people negotiate through this transition they can choose between different paths. Nancy Schlossberg[32] identified six major paths that retirees follow: Continuers, Adventurers, Easy Gliders, Involved Spectators, Searchers, and Retreaters.

Continuers contain with their work identity but may make small tweaks, such as working fewer hours. This is how many start this stage of life. The Adventurers want to try new things and explore childhood aspirations. Easy Gliders are following the traditional path and appreciate the lack of structure as they prioritise relaxation. The Involved Spectators have left their job but haven't let it go and continue to keep up to date with their industry, which may influence their future direction. Searchers are on a quest to find their true calling in retirement. They may eventually settle into more defined paths. Finally, Retreaters take a step back, hoping to figure things out. However, there is a danger that this approach can lead to depression as they lack any purpose. Which can you most relate to?

As you move through the book, we will be considering all the different aspects for a successful retirement – we are going to be the trailblazers for a 21st-century style of retirement that our younger friends aspire to. Exciting times!

Activity 2.6

As we move to the end of this section, let's look at the resources that help with this period. We all bring different strengths to a transition. To what extent

- Are you able to handle the world independently and tolerate uncertainty?
- Do you see the glass as half full or half empty?
- Do you absolve yourself of blame yourself for what happens?
- Do you feel empowered to manage your response to any change?
- Do you believe that your efforts will affect the outcome of a particular course of action?
- Do you have a sense of meaning and purpose?
- Do you exhibit qualities that foster resilience?
- Do you have a support system in place to help you with this transition?

Write down your answers in your journal.

BEFORE YOU MOVE ON ...

Reflect on how much you have learned about transitions and make a note of where you are in the process. Have you found yourself a supporter to keep you on track through this phase; this could be your reflections buddy or someone else. Have you also designed your own ritual or ceremony to take you through this retirement transition. You don't need it fully formed right now but it would be helpful to come up with some thoughts and ideas, and you may get inspiration through a nature walk.

Let's move on to Chapter 3 with some exercises where you reflect on where you are now, what retirement means to you, and your vision for the future.

NOTES

1 Schlossberg, N.K. (1991). *Overwhelmed: Coping with Life's Ups and Downs.* Lexington Books, Lexington, MA.
2 Nuttman-Shwartz, O. (2004). Like a high wave: Adjustment to retirement. *The Gerontologist,* 44, 229–236.
3 Floyd, F.J., Haynes, S.N., Doll, E.R., Winemiller, D., Lemsky, C., Burgy, T.M., et al. (1992). Assessing retirement satisfaction and perceptions of retirement experiences. *Psychology and Aging,* 7, 609–621; and Fouquereau, E., Fernandez, A., Fonseca, A.M., Paul, M.C., & Uotinen, V. (2005). Perceptions of and satisfaction with retirement: A comparison of six European Union countries. *Psychology and Aging,* 20(3), 524–528.
4 Barron, M.L., Streib, G., & Suchman E.A., (1952). Research on the social disorganization of retirement. *American Sociological Review,* 17(4), 479–482.
5 Beehr, T.A., & Bennett, M.M. (2007). Examining retirement from a multilevel perspective. In Shultz, K.A., & Adams, G.A. (Eds.), Retirement: Reasons, processes, and results, 277–302. New York: Springer.
6 Shultz, K.S., & Wang, M. (2011). Psychological perspectives on the changing nature of retirement. *American Psychologist,* 66, 170–179.
7 Kim, J.E., & Moen, P. (2002). Retirement transitions, gender, and psychological well-being: A life-course, ecological model. *Journals of Gerontology: Psychological Sciences,* 57B, 212–222.
8 Richardson, V. E. (1993). *Retirement Counseling: A Handbook for Gerontology Practitioners.* Springer, New York.
9 Wang, M., Henkens, K., & van Solinge, H. (2011). Retirement adjustment: A review of theoretical and empirical advancements. *American Psychologist,* 66(3), 204–213.
10 Festinger, L. (1957). *A Theory of Cognitive Dissonance.* Stanford University Press.

11 Van Solinge, H., & Henkens, K. (2008). Adjustment to and satisfaction with retirement: Two of a kind? *Psychology and Aging*, 23(2), 422–434.

12 Wang et al., Retirement adjustment.

13 Dingemans, E., & Henkens, K. (2015). How do retirement dynamics influence mental well-being in later life? A 10-year panel study. *Scandinavian Journal of Work, Environment & Health*, 41(1), 16–23.

14 Savickas, M.L. (2005). The theory and practice of career construction. In S. D. Brown & R. W. Lent (eds.), *Career Development and Counseling: Putting Theory and Research to Work* (42–70). Wiley, Hoboken, NJ.

15 Bleidorn, W., & Schwaba, T. (2018). Retirement is associated with change in self-esteem. *Psychology and Aging*, 33, 586–594.

16 Burr, A., Santo, J., & Pushkar, D. (2011). Affective well-being in retirement: The influence of values, money, and health across three years. *Journal of Happiness Studies*, 12(1), 17–40.

17 Bosse, R., Aldwin, C.M., Levenson, M.R., & Workman-Daniels, K. (1991). How stressful is retirement? Findings from the normative aging study. *Journal of Gerontology*, 46(1), 9–14.

18 van Solinge, H. (2012). Adjustment to retirement. In M. Wang (ed.), *The Oxford Handbook of Retirement* (311–324). Oxford University Press, Oxford.

19 DWP, YouGov PLC, (2015). DWP ad hoc research report no. 15. *Attitudes of the over 50s to Fuller Working Lives*. ISBN 978-1-78425-432-2.

20 Ashforth, B. (2001). *Role Transitions in Organizational Life: An Identity-based Perspective*. Erlbaum, Mahwah, NJ.

21 van Gennep, A. (1960), *The Rites of Passage*, trans. M. B. Vizedom and G. L. Caffee. University of Chicago Press, Chicago.

22 Bridges, W. (1996). *Managing Transitions: Making the Most of Change*. Nicholas Brealey Publishing, London.

23 Conley, Chip. (2018). *Wisdom at Work: The Making of a Modern Elder*. Penguin.

24 Feiler, B. (2020) *Life Is in the Transitions: Mastering Change at Any Age*. Penguin.

25 Van Solinge & Henkens, Adjustment to and satisfaction with retirement.

26 Schlossberg, *Overwhelmed: Coping with Life's Ups and Downs*.

27 Van Solinge & Henkens, Adjustment to and satisfaction with retirement.

28 Ross, C.E., & Drentea, P. (1998). Consequences of retirement activities for distress and the sense of personal control. *Journal of Health and Social Behavior*, 39, 317–334.

29 Gall, T.L., Evans, D.R., & Howard, J. (1997). The retirement adjustment process: Changes in the well-being of male retirees across time. *Journal of Gerontology: Psychological Sciences*, 52b(3), 110–117.

30 van Solinge, Adjustment to retirement. In *The Oxford Handbook of Retirement*.
31 Wang et al., Retirement adjustment.
32 Schlossberg, N. (2004). *Retire Smart, Retire Happy: Finding Your True Path in Life*. American Psychological Association, Washington, DC.

3

WHERE ARE YOU NOW?

Why you should read this chapter

We discussed transitions in the last chapter; now let's get focused on what retirement means to you, where you are right now, and your vision for the future. This chapter covers the importance of taking stock in different aspects of life. We will start with your most important assets – health, relationships, work and finances, and then move on to others, such as your views of retirement, your interests, and thoughts on ageing. We will finish by a consideration of your future self. There's quite a bit of writing in your journal in this chapter as I'd like you to understand your current position against these areas. You will then be better placed to know where to focus your energy in the near future. For example, if less than satisfied with your health or relationships, what can you do now to address this? Grab your journal and pen and let's get started.

HEALTH

Health is probably our most important asset, more than our finances. This includes both physical and mental health, fitness and wellness. We'll talk more about health and wellbeing in Chapter 6. For now, you may like to answer these questions

DOI: 10.4324/9781003374206-4

Activity 3.1

1. How satisfied are you with your health?
2. How does your health compare to other people of your age?
3. How healthy would you say your diet is?
4. Do you currently smoke? How much?
5. How often do you drink alcohol? How much?
6. How would you rate your mental well-being?
7. Are there any habits you wish to change? What are they?
8. How physically active are you compared with other people your age?
9. Do any health problems restrict the kind of work you can do or your leisure activities?
10. How often do you feel rested when you wake in the morning?
11. Have you seen a doctor or other health professional for a check-up in the past year?
12. What type of activity/exercise do you do and how often do you participate in these activities?
    I.   Light exercise (walking, dancing, or gardening).
    II. Vigorous physical exercise or sport, (aerobics, running, swimming, or cycling).
    III. Weight-bearing exercise.

Overall, how satisfied are you with your health?

Rate yourself on this 1–10 scale (10 is high).

1 – 2 – 3 – 4 – 5 – 6 – 7 – 8 – 9 – 10

Add any reflections and possible action you can take in your journal.

RELATIONSHIPS

We'll talk more about relationships in Chapter 7; for now you may like to consider *all* your relationships. First, there is your relationship with yourself: do you like the person you are? We then look at your close romantic relationship, family, friends, and acquaintances.

Relationships with myself

Activity 3.2

I'd like you to journal on how much you like yourself, using these questions but also being free to write on anything else that this question raises. There is no need to share this with other people; it is for your own benefit.

1. How do you describe your self-image and how has it changed over time?
2. How do you handle negative self-talk and self-criticism?
3. How do you practice self-compassion and self-forgiveness?
4. How do you respond to compliments or positive feedback from others?
5. In what ways do you feel confident and secure in yourself, and in what ways do you feel unsure or vulnerable?
6. What are some things you would like to change or improve in your relationship with yourself?

Relationships with partner/spouse

Activity 3.3

I'd like you to journal about your relationship with your partner/spouse. Ignore this section if it is not relevant to you.

1. What do you appreciate most about your partner/ spouse and why?
2. How do you communicate with each other, both in terms of what you say and how you say it?

3. How do you handle disagreements or conflicts in your relationship?
4. What are your shared interests and values, and how do they influence your relationship?
5. How do you make time for each other and prioritise your relationship amidst the demands of daily life?
6. How do you support and encourage each other in your personal and professional growth?
7. What are some things you would like to improve or change in your relationship and why?
8. How do you deal with stress or challenges as a couple and how does it affect your relationship?
9. What role does trust, honesty, and vulnerability play in your relationship?
10. How do you keep the romance and intimacy alive in your relationship?

You may also like to make a note of any conversation you have had on retirement and how much time you plan to spend together. Couples vary and some like to do most things together, others have their own interests. Neither is better than the other. It's worth taking time to think about how it is right now, and how it will change with retirement. For example, how much alone time will you both want to have each day?

Overall, how satisfied are you with your romantic relationship?

Rate yourself on this 1–10 scale (10 is high).

1 – 2 – 3 – 4 – 5 – 6 – 7 – 8 – 9 – 10

Add any reflections and possible action you can take in your journal.

Relationships with family

Families differ; some are close, many are more distant, and there can be estrangement with one or more members.

Activity 3.4

Consider your relationship with your parents, your children, siblings, wider family. Look at these questions and answer as many as you want in your journal; you don't need to share it with anyone unless you want to.

1. How have your relationships with your family members changed over time, and why?
2. How do you communicate with your family members; what impact does it have on your relationships?
3. What role does family play in your life; how important is it to you?
4. How do you deal with conflicts or challenges within your family; does it affect your relationships?
5. What are the shared values, traditions, and beliefs that define your family; how do they influence your relationships?
6. How do you balance the demands of family with other commitments and responsibilities in your life?
7. What are some things you would like to improve or change in your relationships with your family members and why?
8. How do you support and care for each other as a family; how does it impact your relationships?
9. Who is there for you when you need practical help or emotional support?
10. What role does forgiveness, empathy, and compassion play in your family relationships?

Overall, how satisfied are you with your family relationships?

Rate yourself on this 1–10 scale (10 is high).

1 – 2 – 3 – 4 – 5 – 6 – 7 – 8 – 9 – 10

Add any reflections and possible action you can take in your journal.

Relationships with others – friends, wider social network, colleagues

Activity 3.5

We can be closer to friends than our family or we may struggle to make friends. We may have a large circle of friends going back to school days or just one or two close friends. We may crave a close friendship. Here are a few areas to consider and make a note of in your journal.

1. What role do shared experiences, interests, and values play in your friendships?
2. How do you deal with conflicts or challenges with your friends and how does it affect your relationships?
3. Are there some things you would like to improve or change in your friendships and why?
4. Are there people in your life who accept you just as you are?
5. Do you have friends who can be relied on no matter what happens?
6. Do you have someone you can confide in about things that are important to you?
7. Do you have enough real friends?
8. How would you describe your general social activity now?
9. How socially active are you compared with most people your age?

Overall, how satisfied are you with your wider relationships?

Rate yourself on this 1–10 scale (10 is high).

1 – 2 – 3 – 4 – 5 – 6 – 7 – 8 – 9 – 10

Add any reflections and possible action you can take in your journal.

WORK

Activity 3.6

It's been a big part of your life and will have given you much satisfaction, plus some frustration. You may like to look back at your career history and make a note of:

1. Satisfaction levels with different jobs.
2. Why you chose your career path.
3. What skills and talents you want to keep using.
4. What skills and talents you want to say goodbye to.
5. Any experience of volunteering and/or board membership.
6. Are you considering any paid work? What are you considering?

Again, you can make notes in your journal. This area may be one to discuss with your reflections buddy. We return to this in Chapter 5, where we look at it more broadly to include filling the gap for when you retire.

Overall, how satisfied are you with your working life?

Rate yourself on this 1–10 scale (10 is high).

1 – 2 – 3 – 4 – 5 – 6 – 7 – 8 – 9 – 10

Add any reflections and possible action you can take in your journal.

FINANCIAL WELL-BEING

Activity 3.7

People have different views on how much money is enough for them to feel ok. We'll talk about finances in Chapter 8; for now you may like to answer these questions in your journal:

1. How satisfied are you with your financial situation (retirement savings and pensions)?
2. When you retire, do you expect your living standards to increase, stay about the same, or decrease?
3. How concerned are you with your future financial situation?

Overall, how satisfied are you with finances/financial well-being?

Rate yourself on this 1–10 scale (10 is high).

1 – 2 – 3 – 4 – 5 – 6 – 7 – 8 – 9 – 10

Add any reflections and possible action you can take in your journal.

VIEWS ON RETIREMENT

Activity 3.8

There are a number of questions here. I suggest you make a note of the answers in your journal.

- Where are you on your retirement journey? You could be in your 50s and planning ahead, in your 60s and looking forward to this next stage of life. Or perhaps you have already retired and realise you are drifting.
- How do you feel about leaving work? (Hopeful, dread, anxious, excited?) Why?
- How do you expect that leaving work will affect your life? Make a note of your initial thoughts on: Will leaving work create a gap in your life? Will it make room for taking up things that you've never done before or haven't had time for? Other things?
- How do you think leaving work will affect your spouse's/partner's life?
- Do you think leaving the workforce will affect your childrens' expectations of you?
- Any initial thoughts on how you will define success in retirement?

Activity 3.9

I've now got three short questionnaires for you to complete. You may like to note any thoughts in your journal and discuss your answers with your reflections buddy. You can tick to show your answer against each question. You can also find these, to print out via this page – https://denisetaylor.co.uk/rethinking-retirement/

	Strongly disagree	Disagree	Neutral	Agree	Strongly agree
I look forward to retirement as a pleasant time in life.					
My life after retirement will be very similar to my life now.					
Retirement will be a time to relax.					
Retirement will be the welcome beginning of a new stage of my life.					
Nothing will be able to replace work in my life.					
Retirement will free me from the demands of other people.					
Retirement will be a time to do what I want.					
Most people are happy in retirement.					

Below is a list of things that some people say they look forward to in retirement. For each one please indicate how much you look forward to it.

	Not at all	A little	Quite a lot	A lot	N/A
Less pressure.					
Time just to be (taking things easy).					
Having more time with my spouse/partner.					
Spending more time with my children or grandchildren.					
Time for hobbies or sports.					
Having more time for voluntary work.					
Having the chance to travel.					
Being my own boss.					
A new start.					
Time to create a more meaningful life.					
Time to focus on some big goals.					
To be in control of my own time.					
Sharing wisdom through helping others.					

Now for some things that worry some people about retirement. Please indicate how much they worry you (or maybe not at all).

	Worry a lot	Worry somewhat	Worry a little	Not at all
Feeling too old to do what I want to do.				
Being bored, having too much time on my hands.				
Not doing anything productive or useful.				
Missing people I work with.				
Becoming ill or disabled.				
Not having enough income to get by.				
Inflation and the cost of living.				

INTERESTS

Think of interests in its wider form to include hobbies, leisure pursuits, appreciation for nature and personal/ intellectual development. When we retire, we have more time and there are many possibilities. For now, you may like to think of how you spend your free time and answer these questions, making a note in your journal.

Activity 3.10

1. How do you like to spend your free time and why?
2. What hobbies or interests do you have outside of work?
3. How do you balance leisure activities with responsibilities and chores at home?
4. How do you prioritise self-care and relaxation in your free time?
5. How do you spend time with friends and family, and how important is it to you?
6. What role does exercise or physical activity play in your free time and why?
7. How do you like to spend time outdoors or in nature?
8. What role does learning or personal development play in your free time and why?
9. To what extent do you spend time on activities that challenge your thinking or involve new ideas?
10. What role does travel or adventure play in your free time and why?
11. Do you like to spend time quietly alone; why is this important to you?
12. How happy are you with the balance of time spent on different activities?
13. What new social activities have you taken up in the last year?
14. Have you some ideas of how you want to spend your time when you retire?

Overall, how satisfied are you with your non-working activity?

Rate yourself on this 1–10 scale (10 is high).

1 – 2 – 3 – 4 – 5 – 6 – 7 – 8 – 9 – 10

Add any reflections and possible action you can take in your journal.

VIEWS ON AGEING

Becca Levy[1] has said that our views on ageing can affect how long we will live. A positive attitude can add over seven years to our lifetime. Be honest in your answer to these questions. You will see I've added 'why' to most of them as it is important to dig deeper into our underlying belief about ageing.

Activity 3.11

1. How do you feel about the idea of getting older and why?
2. What are your concerns and fears about ageing, and why?
3. How do you view the ageing process? Do you see it as a natural part of life or as a problem to be overcome?
4. How do you think ageing affects your physical, emotional, and mental well-being, and why?
5. How do you think ageing affects your relationships and social life, and why?
6. What role does ageing play in your career and work life, and why?
7. How do you approach the topic of ageing with friends, family, and loved ones, and why?
8. How do you think society views ageing, and how does it impact your views on ageing?
9. How do you view the potential for personal growth and fulfilment as you age, and why?
10. What role does community and social engagement play in your views on ageing, and why?

MY (BEST POSSIBLE) FUTURE SELF

Do you have a view of what you will be like in five or ten years' time? We will look at this again in Chapter 13; you may like to gather some initial thoughts now so you can refer back later. Review all the areas in this chapter; do you have any expectations on your health, relationships, your money, how you will spend your time?

As we look forward, we could think about the health problems we may well have and the regrets of what we never did.

But does this help? What is helpful is to think about how our life could be in two, five, and ten years' time. Our best possible self.[2] What will we be doing, living, how will our relationships be, what will give us meaning? Who can we help and support, and who will be there for us? What activities will engage our body and mind?

Activity 3.12

Close your eyes and imagine yourself five years older than you are now and make a note in your journal. Then do the same for ten years into the future. Here are my notes.

> In five years', time I see myself doing more of the same. I'm still living in a three-storey house, still being active. I've lost a little weight and am definitely fitter now. I'm stronger and enjoy lifting weights. I continue to work and have had two more books published but I am more choosy about the time spent on work to allow more time for writing. Still living with my partner and appreciating that you need to put time into a relationship and to compromise. I'm happy in five years' time.

> Ten years into the future and I've been working hard on losing weight as I'm now noticing more pains. The stairs have got too much for me, but I didn't want 'bungalow legs' so we have moved to a two-storey house, and we have a cleaner as I no longer want to fight with the duvet or clean the kitchen and bathroom. I still do some work and it keeps my brain active. Alas, my mother has died so I'm now the eldest of my family and arranging family events.

BEFORE YOU MOVE ON …

There has been much thinking and reflection in this chapter, I have a habit of skimming over to come back to things later, and I never do … I encourage you to take some time and answer these questions so you can refer to them as we move on to further consideration in the upcoming chapters. I'd also like you to consider your approach to journalling. Journalling is a form of noticing and so, as well as reflecting on the activities, I'd like you to spend a bit more time noticing things. When you go outside, what do you notice on a walk? Consider the inside you: have you noticed any changes to your mood and feelings? Is there anything you notice in the media that has impacted on you? It can be helpful to go into more detail on what you notice around you and inside you as well as following the prompts I've included.

NOTES

1 Levy, B. (2022) *Breaking the Age Code*. Ebury.
2 Carrillo, A., Martínez-Sanchis, M., Etchemendy, E., & Baños, R.M. (2019). Qualitative analysis of the best possible self intervention: Underlying mechanisms that influence its efficacy. *PLoS One*, 14(5).

4

WHO ARE YOU?
(PSYCHOLOGICAL FACTORS)

Why you should read this chapter

As we age it is even more important to understand the person that we are. Carl Jung has written much on later life including: "Looking outwards has got to be turned into looking into oneself. Discovering yourself provides you with all you are, were meant to be, and all you are living from and for". This chapter helps you to understand more about your personality, values, passion. We look at being proactive, optimism, self-esteem, self-efficacy, and mastery. We then consider social identity and the impact of groups on who we are. We don't need to accept the 'retired identity' unless we choose to.

Most people love finding out about who they are and, for over 35 years, that's what I've been doing in my work: helping people to get an in-depth understanding of themselves, mainly so they can be more effective at work. Over the past few years, I've taken a different approach; instead of helping people to fit in with what was expected of them in the workplace, I've focused on helping clients to understand more about their natural style, their usual way of being, their authentic self. This focus on inner development is a way of becoming more fulfilled. Life becomes so much easier when we don't need to try to be anyone else and we can be our natural, authentic selves.

Psychological factors have an impact in many different areas of our life, such as after physical illness, relocation transition, cross-cultural adjustment, and transition to parenthood. The

DOI: 10.4324/9781003374206-5

most common psychological factors are personality character-istics, and these have been found to influence the extent to which positive outcomes occur as people adjust to life transi-tions such as marriage, divorce, and career choice.[1]

There are many factors that influence an individual's adjust-ment to retirement. While there is a wealth of research that examines the role of health and financial security, less is known about the role of psychological factors. In this chapter we are going to look at some specific ones. My research started with a systematic review (where research is conducted into all studies based on specific terms) where I looked deep into this topic. Based on an initial review of over 12,000 studies, I care-fully read 106 academic papers (and got very good at speed reading!) and the final review included almost 11,000 people. This revealed seven broad psychological factors that have been examined in relation to retirement adjustment: personality, values, self-esteem, self-efficacy, mastery, social identity, and calling, which are covered in this chapter.

This is a big chapter, divided into sections. I take each per-sonality factor in turn, explain what they are, you take a view on how you measure up, and I make suggestions on actions you could take if you want to make changes. There will also be final thoughts from me.

I'm not looking for you to be a perfect match on each one; it is in our understanding of where, for example we may be low, that we can be better prepared if that personality factor is ever needed, with suggestions on what to do next. We also can help others best, and be more satisfied in our work and relationships, if we understand who we are, and what triggers may impact on us.

PERSONALITY

Personality theory can be useful in the study of retirement adjust-ment as it makes predictions about both behaviour and subjec-tive experiences.[2] A popular way of measuring personality is an assessment that looks at the 'Big Five' factors which are: open-ness to experience (O), conscientiousness (C), extraversion (E), agreeableness (A), and neuroticism (N). Easy to remember as OCEAN. These are all broad personality traits that consist of a number of behaviours and motivations. You can access a free version of this assessment via this link, which was working as this book went to publication – https://bigfive-test.com. There are 120 questions to answer, and it should take about ten minutes. Your results are shown as six sub-scales of each factor and you can save your results and compare against other groups.

Various researchers,[3] looked at the links between the Big Five personality traits, reasons for retirement, and the experience of being retired, and found that high conscientiousness, high agreeableness, and low neuroticism (particularly the depression and vulnerability sub-scales), were all related to retirement satisfaction. Extraversion correlated as a positive outcome for retirees; when someone is high in extraversion it is linked to more involvement in social and leisure activities.[4,5]

In all these studies, whilst there was support for the personality traits of high levels of conscientiousness, agreeableness, extraversion, and low neuroticism, openness was not identified in any of the studies. One explanation could be that openness is best treated as a value;[6] values will be covered in the next section.

Although many think that personality is fixed, it isn't and can change. There is ample evidence indicating that our personalities are not static. Typically, we experience changes across all five dimensions of the Big Five personality traits from the ages of 20 to 40. As we move into the subsequent two decades, we tend to become increasingly emotionally stable and conscientious. As we pass the age of 60, our conscientiousness tends to gradually increase, while our openness and extroversion tend to decrease. Of course, this is generalised; you may be different. Also, as we become more open to being who we are, and more truthful in our responses, we can see a difference to when we completed assessments to get a promotion or as part of the recruitment process.

One study[7] found that after retirement, participants described themselves as less fast-paced and vigorous as well as less competitive and argumentative than before. It may well be that when completing an assessment, we think of our ideal self in the workplace rather than the 'shoes-off self' we would rather be. For those who don't change, they may find that a personality suited to work may not be a personality suited to retirement. If you are a high achiever, keen to do well, and to push for your own goals, you will demonstrate lower agreeableness and higher extraversion.

Let's now look at these five personality factors in the OCEAN order.

Activity 4.1 – complete the assessment

Time to stop and complete the assessment so you can look at your results as you read on. Here is the link – https://bigfive-test.com.

Openness

Openness is a multidimensional construct that includes various facets such as openness to experience, intellect, and a general appreciation for art, emotion, adventure, unusual ideas, imagination, curiosity. One sub-trait is around emotionality and awareness of your feelings, another is adventurousness: wanting to try out new experiences and to avoid routine. The sub-scale of liberalism is around challenge of authority and traditional values.

People who score high in openness tend to be more creative, curious, and open-minded. They are more likely to be interested in exploring new ideas, experiences, and ways of thinking. They also tend to be more imaginative, enjoy beauty and nature, and appreciate art and aesthetics. However, this does not mean that they are disconnected from reality or that they prefer fantasy over facts. Whilst high scorers in openness are more likely to be interested in intellectual pursuits and may question traditional values, this is only part of this trait.

Activity 4.2 – your self-assessment of openness

Has a review of your results told you anything new or confirmed what you know? Are there some areas that you would like to change? Perhaps you would like to challenge some rules and start to take adventures, but something holds you back? Perhaps you would like to be more open and to widen your interest in the arts?

Make a note of any action you could take. For example, watching some programmes on Sky Arts, taking time to name how you are feeling. Perhaps you challenge too much, and you could consider why some rules should be followed.

Conscientiousness

Conscientiousness is a personality trait that is characterised by being organised, responsible, self-disciplined, and goal-oriented. As such, individuals who score high on the conscientiousness scale may be more likely to adopt healthier and more active lifestyles during retirement.[8]

Research has shown that high levels of conscientiousness are associated with engaging in post-retirement volunteering[9] and cognitively stimulating activities, such as playing card games and doing puzzles.[10] These activities can help maintain cognitive function and provide a sense of purpose and social connection in retirement.

Conscientiousness includes several sub-traits, including self-efficacy, orderliness, dutifulness, self-discipline, and achievement-striving. Self-efficacy refers to the belief in one's ability to accomplish tasks and achieve goals. Orderliness is about being organised and having a structured approach to life. Dutifulness is about having a strong sense of responsibility and moral obligation. Self-discipline is about exercising willpower and ensuring that tasks are completed. Achievement-striving is about setting high standards for oneself and striving for excellence.

While high levels of conscientiousness can be beneficial for post-retirement well-being, it is also important to maintain a healthy balance. Being too high in achievement-striving can lead to an unhealthy obsession with work and difficulty letting go, which can negatively impact retirement experiences. It is important to find a balance that allows for continued growth and engagement while also enjoying the benefits of retirement.

Activity 4.3 – your self-assessment of conscientiousness

As you look at your results you can consider how true this is for you. Have you always been organised and self-disciplined? Has something changed how you usually are?

Make a note of any action you could take. Would it help to take a more organised approach with greater self-discipline and if this doesn't come easy, how can you make the change. As we move into this next stage of life, we can create a plan, and follow the plan, but some may be too fixated on the plan and treat it like a work task. Would it be helpful to let go and to be open to what may be?

Extraversion

Extraversion is a personality trait that is characterised by sociability, assertiveness, talkativeness, and a tendency to seek out and enjoy social interactions.[11] It is around how we engage with the external world. Individuals who score high on the extraversion scale may be more likely to actively seek out new experiences and opportunities, including those related to retirement.

There is more to this scale than being outgoing. Introverts should not be seen as shy; they just need less external stimulation. This scale includes friendliness and reaching out to others. We should be aware that there are both confident and unconfident versions of introverts and extraverts. It has been said that Margaret Thatcher (ex UK Prime Minister) was a confident introvert. One reason for extraverts being sociable is that they fear loneliness and rejection, whilst introverts fear chaos.

In the context of retirement, being extraverted may help individuals to stay active and engaged during the transition from work to retirement. This could include pursuing new hobbies or interests, volunteering, or engaging in social activities. Additionally, because extraverts tend to be more outgoing and sociable, they may find it easier to establish new friendships and social connections during retirement.

Extraverts may also be better equipped to navigate retirement-related institutions and interactions, such as dealing with financial advisors, healthcare providers, and government agencies. Their natural assertiveness and confidence may help them to advocate for themselves and ensure that they are receiving the best possible care and services. Extraverts are likely to have busy lives and take an energetic approach to life. Some seek excitement and will take risks.

Gregariousness includes the excitement of crowds, but not everyone wants to have a lot of contact with others. I am happy to spend time with people, I come across as warm and friendly, but I also avoid crowds and appreciate much time alone. The final sub-scale is cheerfulness and measures mood and feelings.

Extraverts tend to have a more positive outlook on life and enjoy social interactions, and so may view the whole retirement experience more positively as an opportunity for growth and new experiences rather than as a period of decline or loss. Of course, everyone's experience of retirement is unique, and many factors beyond personality traits can influence how individuals adjust to this major life transition.

Activity 4.4 – your self-assessment of extraversion

You may be surprised by your result. I see myself as an introvert but came high on this extraversion scale. Whilst I get on well with people, I prefer one-to-one situations or groups I know well; I also need a lot of personal quiet time to recharge. As you look at your results, you can consider if you have been true to yourself or are still trying to fit in with the work you. You may like to journal around this. James was surprised that his score was lower than he anticipated, but it was down to some stressful events in his life, and the results are only a snapshot. He planned to take this assessment again as his situation improved.

Make a note of any action you could take. Do you have enough contact with people, and enough time alone? What balance is right for you? How is your mood at the moment and how typical is that over the longer term?

Agreeableness

Agreeableness refers to the extent to which a person is cooperative, empathetic, and concerned about others' well-being. They also tend to value social harmony and avoid conflict. Trust is the extent to which a person believes that others have good intentions. High scorers tend to be more optimistic and willing to take risks in social situations. Morality is the extent to which a person is honest, fair, and candid with others. High scorers in morality tend to be more ethical and principled. Altruism is the extent to which a person is genuinely interested in helping others. High scorers in altruism tend to be more compassionate, empathetic, and selfless. Cooperation is the extent to which a person is willing to compromise and work with others to achieve common goals. High scorers in cooperation tend to be more diplomatic and conciliatory. Finally, modesty is the extent to which a person is humble and unassuming. It is not related to agreeableness in a straightforward way, but people who score high in modesty tend to be less assertive and more deferential to others.

Activity 4.5 – your self-assessment of agreeableness

Do you see yourself as a 'people pleaser' who avoids conflict. At times, do you wish that you put your needs first? In the workplace, a lower score can be required if we need to make objective and tough decisions; is this what is needed for this next life stage?

Make a note of any action you could take if you would like to move your score. Would you like to be more trusting of others, and how could you change. If you score high does this mean that you are sometimes taken advantage of? You can also think of what you can do to move your score lower.

Neuroticism

Neuroticism refers to the tendency to experience negative feelings and is based on several dimensions. Anxiety refers to the extent to which a person experiences feelings of worry and fear. High scorers in anxiety tend to be more tense and nervous, while low scorers tend to be calmer and more relaxed. Anger refers to the extent to which a person experiences feelings of irritation and frustration. High scorers in anger tend to be more easily annoyed and prone to outbursts, while low scorers tend to be more patient and forgiving.

Depression refers to the extent to which a person experiences feelings of sadness, hopelessness, and lack of energy. High scorers in depression tend to be more prone to negative thoughts and feelings, while low scorers tend to be more optimistic and energetic. Self-consciousness refers to the extent to which a person is sensitive to what others think of them. High scorers in self-consciousness tend to be more self-critical and concerned about social evaluation, while low scorers tend to be more confident and self-assured.

Immoderation refers to the extent to which a person is prone to impulsive behaviour and strong cravings. High scorers in immoderation tend to be more prone to addiction and other problematic behaviours, while low scorers tend to be more self-disciplined and able to control their impulses. Vulnerability refers to the extent to which a person is sensitive to stress and prone to experiencing negative emotions. High scorers in vulnerability tend to be more reactive to stress and more prone to anxiety and other negative emotions, while low scorers tend to be more resilient and able to cope with stress more effectively.

Activity 4.6 – your self-assessment of neuroticism

As you look at your results you can consider if this is triggered by your current situation, as you approach or are in the midst of change. Is it clear what is making you feel anxious or depressed or can you not put your finger on the reasons why? Are you feeling stressed because you are uncertain about the future, many things are outside of our control? So, consider what you can control.

Would you like to be less anxious about situations? Less bothered about what others think. If a person or situation is making you feel angry, but you hold this into yourself, would therapy or an active way of expressing this anger be helpful? Is there something currently triggering you so that you are feeling more depressed and self-conscious? Are you being brought down by uncertainty – it may help to journal around what you can control and focus on those things.

Bringing things together

Many studies document strong associations between the traits of Extraversion and emotional stability (low Neuroticism) on the one hand and self-reports of happiness, subjective well-being, and overall psychological adjustment among adults on the other.[12,13] Indeed, current thinking on these traits of extraversion and neuroticism suggests that these broad dimensions of personality should be associated with well-being through all stages of our lives. The broad traits of conscientiousness and agreeableness can also show positive associations with psychological well-being and correlate with prosocial involvements in adulthood such as community volunteerism.[14,15] People should become more dominant, agreeable, conscientious, and emotionally stable over the course of adult life, and in particular at this life stage.[16] How well does this description suit you?

There is more to personality than the 'Big Five'. We will shortly consider the proactive personality and optimism before looking at wider factors such as self-esteem, self-efficacy, and values.

Combining personality characteristics

Personality traits can influence the total resources an individual has as they approach retirement. These personality traits can have an impact on a range of factors, including financial preparedness, reasons for retirement, and the need for a disability pension. Studies have found that personality traits such as extraversion, conscientiousness, and neuroticism can be linked to various aspects of retirement preparation and adjustment. For example, extraverted individuals may have more social support during the retirement transition, while conscientious individuals may be better prepared for retirement and enjoy better health in later life. In contrast, neurotic individuals may be less prepared for retirement and may have less social support during the transition.

We don't look at personality traits in isolation but combine them together into types.[17] Studies have identified three personality types: resilients, under-controllers, and over-controllers. You may like to consider which you can relate to.

Resilients are often characterised by particularly low scores on neuroticism and high scores on other traits such as extraversion, conscientiousness, openness, and agreeableness. Resilients are typically adaptable, optimistic, and able to cope with stressors effectively. They tend to have high levels of well-being and experience favourable outcomes in most studies.

Under-controllers often score low on openness, conscientiousness, and agreeableness, and may lack self-discipline, responsibility, and empathy. They may engage in risky behaviours, exhibit aggressive tendencies, and have difficulty forming positive relationships. Studies have found that under-controllers show differential negative effects in various areas of life, such as academic achievement, career success, and mental health.

Over-controllers score low on extraversion but high on neuroticism. They may have a tendency towards anxiety, worry, and self-doubt, and may also be overly cautious and avoidant of risk. Over-controllers may struggle with decision-making, taking action, and forming social connections. In some studies, over-controllers have been found to experience negative outcomes, such as anxiety and depression.

The proactive personality

Even more important than the 'Big Five' personality traits to a positive adjustment to retirement is to what extent someone has a proactive personality. This refers to a set of traits that are characterised by high levels of initiative, self-direction, and a tendency to seek out opportunities for growth and change. People with a proactive personality are generally more likely to take an active role in shaping their environment, rather than simply reacting to it.[18]

Research has shown that having a proactive personality can be particularly important for people during the transition to retirement. Retirement can be a challenging time, as people are faced with major changes in their daily routines and social connections. However, for people with a proactive personality, retirement can also be an opportunity to explore new interests and activities, and to develop new social connections and relationships. Studies have found that people with a proactive personality tend to have higher levels of life satisfaction and well-being, both before and after retirement. For example, a study[19] found that retirees with a proactive personality were more likely to report high levels of life satisfaction and positive emotions and were less likely to experience negative emotions such as anxiety and depression.

My personal reflection

From my research, the most favourable personality characteristics for a successful retirement adjustment are to be high in extraversion, agreeableness and conscientiousness and low in neuroticism along with generativity (covered in Chapter 5 and 9) and the proactive personality. Personally, I can demonstrate extraversion, but I am also self-sufficient and happy to be on my own. For example, I would attend a gig alone if no one else wanted to come with me, but I would get chatting to other fans for some of the time. I'm seen by others as warm and friendly and take an optimistic view of life. Whilst I don't follow all rules if I don't see them as valid, I put task first, and set out to meet my goals and be punctual for meeting people.

Whilst I have suffered from stress, depression, and anxiety in the past, I'm now more likely to be calm – well, most of the time. I also have an optimistic personality, indeed, a previous boss used this as a 'put down' to me. The proactive personality really sums up my personal style: keen to take the initiative and focused on achieving goals. I look ahead and anticipate problems. At this stage of life, I'm stepping up to the role of 'wise elder' and beginning to consider more about future generations and, more widely, the planet.

Activity 4.7 – how do you measure up?

To what extent do you have a proactive personality? How many of these statements do you agree with?

	Strongly disagree	Disagree	Neutral	Agree	Strongly agree
I proactively take action to complete tasks.	1	2	3	4	5
I identify opportunities for improvement.	1	2	3	4	5
If I believe in something I will make it happen.	1	2	3	4	5
I set high targets for myself.	1	2	3	4	5
I am confident in my ability to succeed.	1	2	3	4	5
I am passionate about turning ideas into reality.	1	2	3	4	5
I focus on achieving my goals despite opposition from others.	1	2	3	4	5
I seek a positive outcome in a new situation.	1	2	3	4	5

Your self-assessment

Review your answers to these questions. The higher your score, the more you measure to the proactive personality. If you have been proactive throughout your career, you are likely to continue in this transition to later life.

Proactive behaviour can be learned. What can help is to focus on goal setting and a focus on your future plans. After looking at your results, make a note of any action you could take. If you are not proactive, you may benefit from talking through possibilities with others, both to identify and to see how you can follow through. If this doesn't come easy to you, working with a retirement coach can help.

Optimism

Optimism is one of the most widely researched personality traits[20] and optimism will help us to have a successful retirement. People who are optimistic expect good things to happen. They deal better with negative events and are less likely to suffer from depression and anxiety. They are better at solving problems, and, most importantly, there is increased longevity. A study looking at two cohorts of men and women found that men in the highest versus the lowest quartile of optimism had a 10.9 per cent longer lifespan and had 1.7 greater chance of living to age 85; with women the difference was even greater, with a difference of 14.9 per cent for a longer life.[21]

A systematic review (where research is conducted into all studies based on a specific term) looked at the association between optimism and risk for the likelihood of future cardiovascular events. They found that optimism was associated with a lower risk of cardiovascular events and pessimism with higher risks, and so optimism is an important factor in preventative health.[22]

An optimist is more likely to look on the bright side and see the positive from a situation, and we can increase our optimism levels by expressing gratitude; this is one reason why many people will keep a gratitude diary and is something you may like to do.

Gratitude diary

A gratitude diary is a tool used to help you focus on the positive aspects of your life and cultivate a sense of gratitude. It involves regularly reflecting on the things you are thankful for and writing them down in a journal. You decide on the frequency and time of day and reflect on things that you are thankful for, which can include your health, your job, your family, your friends, or even something as simple as a beautiful sunset. As this becomes a regular habit, over time you will find that focusing on the positive things in your life will help you feel happier and more content.

Many people have found it beneficial to create a habit of noting three things they are grateful for each day; another approach is to reflect on gratitude weekly. You may want to try both options and see which one resonates better for you. For example, you could choose a specific day of the week, such as Saturday morning or Sunday evening. When reflecting on gratitude, it's important to go beyond simply making a bullet list, but to add more detail about what specifically we are grateful for. Writing about people can have more impact than writing about things, and it's also important to look out for the unexpected, as these experiences often have a richness to them. You may find it valuable to discuss your approach with your reflections buddy and also to share and discuss your entries.

Being pessimistic can be detrimental to our health; a more optimistic view can add an extra seven years to our lives.[23] If you tend to look on the dark side, why not begin to notice the times you make a negative comment on something, to identify times when you say that you can't do something and start to change this around. Martin Seligman[24] introduced the concept of learned optimism, where we can change our attitudes and behaviours by acknowledging the positives in our lives and recognising and challenging negative perspectives.

If you are calling yourself a lazy so-and-so, you can reframe it as 'Today I didn't get as much done as I wanted'. Be kinder to yourself and say, 'I will create a list of what to do tomorrow'. You can also start noting in your journal positive events in your life, such as when you helped someone. Consider, too, the people that surround you; if they tend to be negative, it is hard to be different. If you can, find other people to hang out with or work with, and, until then, be willing to challenge them.

If you are more of a glass-half-empty person or if you have fears that hold you back you could give them an actual name, such as 'Fred', so when the fears appear you can tell 'Fred' to go away; it really helps if you start dwelling on negative things from your past.

Activity 4.8 – reflect on optimism

Is this an area where you should focus? I've made some suggestions above on how to become more optimistic. Which of these do you want to use first? It's helpful to write about your progress in your journal so you can see changes made.

SELF ESTEEM

Self-esteem refers to an individual's overall evaluation of themselves and their self-worth, which can have a significant impact on their attitudes towards various aspects of life, including retirement. Studies have shown that individuals with higher levels of self-esteem tend to have more positive attitudes towards retirement and are more likely to experience retirement satisfaction.[25]

Higher self-esteem can help individuals view retirement as an opportunity to explore new interests, develop new skills, and pursue activities that they may not have had time for previously. It can also help individuals maintain a positive outlook on life, even in the face of challenges related to retirement, such as changes in social connections and financial constraints.

Activity 4.9 – reflect on your self worth

You may like to answer these questions to get an understanding of your sense of self-worth:

1. I feel that I have a number of good qualities.
2. I feel that I'm a person of worth, at least on an equal basis with others.
3. I take a positive attitude towards myself.

As you consider your answers to the three questions above, you may like to reflect on why you agreed, or not, with each question. As self-esteem is associated with higher levels of life satisfaction, if your answers were more negative, consider why you score this way. It could be down to a lack of confidence and any work to increase levels of self-esteem whilst still employed could be beneficial both in the workplace and later in retirement. A coach or a course may be helpful for you.

My personal reflection

Past research suggests that late adulthood is characterised by minor declines in self-esteem – not something I recognise within myself. My friend Arthur said just how much I have 'blossomed and grown' since he met me, soon after I started going to watch bands with a 'meetup' group. You may like to reflect on any changes you have noticed in yourself.

SELF-EFFICACY

Self-efficacy is a concept introduced by psychologist Albert Bandura,[26] which refers to an individual's belief in their ability to perform a specific task or handle a particular situation successfully. Self-efficacy beliefs can have a significant impact on an individual's motivation, behaviour, and overall well-being.[27] It has an impact on many areas of our life, such as when we experience burnout at work,[28] and for high performance as an athlete.[29]

Studies have shown that high levels of retirement self-efficacy are positively related to retirement satisfaction and negatively related to feelings of anxiety and depression. Individuals who express anxiety about retirement are more likely to have difficulties adjusting to retirement. In contrast, workers with higher scores on self-efficacy are much more likely to adjust easily to retirement. Adjustment to retirement can be influenced by various factors, such as part-time work, shorter work histories, and our overall perception of retirement as an opportunity rather than a loss. This book is to guide you to have an easier adjustment.

Overall, self-efficacy is an important aspect of an individual's psychological makeup and can significantly influence their adjustment to retirement and overall well-being.

Activity 4.10 – reflect on your self-efficacy

You can get an understanding of your own position through considering how well you agree with these statements:

1. I see myself as resilient.
2. My resourcefulness helps me handle the unexpected.
3. I can solve difficult problems even when they are not easy ones.
4. I have the self-belief that I will achieve my goals.
5. When faced with opposition I generally get my own way.
6. I have developed good ways of coping with life events.

Your self-assessment

Are your results expected? Has anything affected you of late? What helps build higher levels of self-efficacy is to develop resilience, so, if your answers were more negative, you could take some time to reflect on situations that have called for resilience. Consider what helped and, if it didn't go so well, what you have learned from it. It can help to have good role models and to read stories and to talk with people who have made a successful adaptation to this new stage of life. Talking with your reflections buddy may introduce you to some new role models.

MASTERY

Mastery is an important resource in later life[30] and refers to the extent to which individuals believe they can control the outcomes of their lives, rather than being ruled by external forces.[31] This sense of control can have a significant impact on how individuals adjust to retirement and how they cope with stressors in general.

Studies have shown that high levels of mastery are linked to better well-being and can help individuals maintain a sense of control and purpose in their lives.[32] Mastery can include both self-efficacy and locus of control, which refers to an individual's perception of the degree to which they can control the outcomes of their lives.

Retirement can be a significant life transition, and individuals who have a strong sense of mastery are more likely to successfully adjust to retirement and find satisfaction in their later years. The sense of control that comes with mastery can also help individuals cope with stressors in general, including those related to ageing, health, and social support.

Activity 4.11 – reflect on your level of mastery

You can get an understanding of your own position through considering how well you agree with these statements:

1. What happens to me in the future mostly depends on me.
2. I am in control of my life.
3. I am able to solve more of the problems I have.
4. Nobody tells me what to do.
5. I have inner strength.

Your self-assessment

Do you rate yourself as someone with low or high mastery? As people who report higher mastery tend to report greater retirement adjustment, it can be helpful to think of examples of where you have achieved mastery in other aspects of your life, as this should help with your adjustment. As mastery, along with self-efficacy, gives people inner strength, understanding your role in past successes and what was learned from failure will be helpful. Take some time to write down any examples in your journal and you may like to share with your buddy.

VALUES

Personality traits and values are different constructs. Rokeach[33] has argued that personality traits come before values as they are products of nature, whereas values are learned from how we interact with the environment. The difference can be explained as 'traits refer to what people are like, values to what people consider important'.[34]

Values are the fundamental beliefs that guide us, and understanding our values is important to help us have clarity on what drives us. Our values are not fixed and will change over time. For example, excitement is more important to adolescents, and declines with age; also, our values become more important as we age.[35]

Finding an old values exercise from ten years ago, it was interesting to see that I have moved away from top values of achievement, advancement, initiative, and status to very different top values, to include autonomy, freedom, and wisdom – all useful and relevant to this stage of life.

By retirement, our values should be clearer, and we should be more likely to live in line with our values, especially when we no longer have to 'fit in' with the workplace. Preparing and adjusting for retirement will be helped by an understanding of our values, with greater clarity on what drives us and the impact it has on our lives. This can help to alleviate some of the negative effects of poor health and limited financial resources in our adjustment to retirement.[36]

It's useful to understand our values and there are many lists of values online and some free online assessments (e.g., – https://personalvalu.es/) you could take). You might like to complete the assessment being truly you, not out to impress, and then to compare your results to how you are in your current job (if still working). For most of my clients there is a big mismatch; at work they are having to work outside of their true values. As we move to this retirement transition, we can make choices that are aligned with our beliefs.

Activity 4.12 – complete a values exercise and note your top values

Certain values are more beneficial for the well-being of retirees. My research showed the importance of values in retirement adjustment, with full retirees experiencing stronger increases in openness to change, autonomy, and harmonious passion. I discuss these in more detail now.

I'm not intending that you to take on values that don't resonate with you, but that you understand more about the differences, as it helps with our understanding of other people. Some of us will move into a new relationship later in life and an understanding of our values helps us to understand the differences between us and to appreciate the other person.

Openness to change

If you have high openness-to-change values you are likely to value self-direction, stimulation, and hedonism.[37] The openness-to-change value is focused on flexibility, creativity, independence, and pleasure and enhances positive emotions, protects against negative emotions, and is linked to seeking emotionally meaningful goals.[38] Higher transcendence, which involves concern for the welfare of others and of the natural world, and conservation values predicted more positive emotions. If you are low on openness to change, you are more likely to prefer the conservation values of security, conformity, and tradition.

Autonomy

Autonomy is concerned with the amount of freedom we have to make choices. To what extent do you feel a sense of choice and freedom in the things you do rather than feel obligated with the things you need to do each day? How much pressure comes from other people? The degree of control that individuals have over their retirement decisions and activities can help individuals feel more empowered and engaged in their retirement. People low in autonomy can feel constrained by family and work responsibilities to do what they want to do; they can also feel held back by money and health constraints.

Full-time retirees experience stronger increases in autonomy than those who continue working.[39] This is to be expected, as we have more flexibility and freedom when we are not having to fit in with an organisational way of working. Most gains in autonomy were when people had worked in jobs with low intrinsic work motivation, which may be interpreted as a relief from dissatisfying jobs.

Passion

Do you have a passionate interest? Being passionate about work can lead to positive or negative outcomes in retirement, depending on whether the passion is harmonious or obsessive, respectively.[40] A healthy passion can increase our levels of satisfaction in retirement, and it could be that passionate workers transpose their passion for work to another activity after retirement through undertaking new activities once we retire; and they can fully commit to other activities that are non-passion inspired. An obsessive passion is around a relentless pursuit that takes over ones' life and can lead to feeling of guilt and shame or burnout.

Activity 4.13 – your self-assessment

Have you completed a values exercise? Make a note of your top ones in your journal and date them so you can refer to them again. If retired, it can be helpful to consider to what extent you lived in line with your values when working. And what about now? We no longer have to fit in but can be true to who we are.

We will be looking more at hobbies and interests in Chapter 5. For now, you may like to make a note in your journal of any passionate interests you are currently pursuing and any that interest you.

SOCIAL IDENTITY

Social identity is part of an individual's self-concept that comes from membership of a social group or groups and provides a person with an emotional attachment.[41] When we identify as part of a group, the group becomes part of our personal identity.[42] Satisfaction with retirement is linked to being a member of a group of people who are also retired.[43] However, after full-time work, to what extent do you want to identify as part of a group called 'retired'? It may be there is another group that resonates more with you.

In retirement we can feel a loss of who we are in relationship to other people. We know what we mean by being an accountant, engineer, or teacher, but once we retire, we lose our identity, wonder who we are, and will seek to find a new identity. I cover this in more detail in the next chapter, where I look at how we fill the gap from work, but here it is about how we define ourselves, through the groups we belong to.

What does it mean to be retired? The retiree-identity[44] can take some time to feel right for us. Some people may want to define us as retired. Whilst some are happy to take on this label and that is how they will introduce themselves to others, it is not right for everyone. We don't have to accept what anyone else says, we don't have to go along with a label that has been created by others. We can choose our own, like a made-to-measure suit or pair of shoes.

As we get ready for this stage, we may want to find relevant groups to join to help construct a new identity and you may like to search for a group you can relate to rather than feeling it has to be a specific group. With the importance of social relationships, belonging to several groups is likely to mean that you have the resources to help you in challenging times.[45]

Lucy was highly involved with her work and had no outside interests. Discussing this was a 'wakeup call' to connect with people outside of drinks after work with colleagues. We identified three possible groups, including a samba drumming group, to see which one most resonated with her, with backups to get involved with when she got more time. She explored these in advance of retirement to enable her to start connecting with people sooner.

Activity 4.14 – actions you could take

Make a note of any groups you belong to and how strongly you feel connected to each group. We will be returning to this topic in Chapter 5. You may also like to make a note in your journal of what retirement means to you.

Activity 4.15 – write a description that reflects your personality

As a final activity you may like to summarise everything you have found out about your personality on to one page.

BEFORE YOU MOVE ON ...

This is a big chapter, and there is much to take in; I hope you found it fascinating. Gaining a deeper understanding of who we are is a great way of becoming all we are meant to be and to truly embrace moving forward in our life. Take a moment to make a note of how your personality has changed over your life. Did you adapt to fit in? What happened when you were more of yourself? In your journal, note changes as you move ahead in life.

NOTES

1 Page, J., Bruch, M.A., & Haase, R.F. (2008). Role of perfectionism and five-factor model traits in career indecision. *Personality and Individual Differences,* 45, 811–815.

2 Ryan, L.H., Newton, N.J., Chauhan, P.K., & Chopik, W.J. (2017). Effects of pre-retirement personality, health and job lock on post-retirement subjective well-being. *Translational Issues in Psychological Science,* 3(4), 378–387.

3 Robinson, O.C., Demetre, J.D., & Corney, R. (2010). Personality and retirement: Exploring the links between the Big Five personality traits, reasons for retirement and the experience of being retired. *Personality and Individual Differences,* 48(7), 792–797.

4 Jopp, D.S., & Hertzog, C. (2010). Assessing adult leisure activities: An extension of a self-report activity questionnaire. *Psychological Assessment,* 22, 108–120.

5 Stephan, Y., Boiché, J., Canada, B., & Terracciano, A. (2014). Association of personality with physical, social, and mental activities across the lifespan: Findings from US and French samples. *British Journal of Psychology,* 105, 564–580.

6 Burr, A., Santo, J., & Pushkar, D. (2011). Affective well-being in retirement: The influence of values, money, and health across three years. *Journal of Happiness Studies,* 12(1), 17–40.

7 Löckenhoff, C.E., Terracciano, A., & Costa Jr., P.T. (2009). Five-factor model personality traits and the retirement transition: Longitudinal and cross-sectional associations. *Psychology and Aging*, 24(3), 722–728.

8 Ryan et al., Effects of pre-retirement personality, health and job lock on post-retirement subjective well-being.

9 Mike, A., Jackson J.J., & Oltmanns T.F. (2014) The conscientious retiree: The relationship between conscientiousness, retirement, and volunteering. *Journal of Research in Personality*, 52, 68–77.

10 Jopp & Hertzog, Assessing adult leisure activities.

11 Reis, M., & Gold, D.P. (1993). Retirement, personality, and life satisfaction: A review and two models. *The Journal of Applied Gerontology*, 12, 261–282.

12 Clark, L. A., & Watson, D. (2008). Temperament: An organizing paradigm for trait psychology. In O.P. John, R.W. Robins, & L.A. Pervin (Eds.), *Handbook of Personality: Theory and Research* (265–286). The Guilford Press.

13 Mroczek, D.K., & Almeida, D.M. (2004). The effect of daily stress, personality, and age on daily negative affect. *Journal of Personality*, 72(2), 355–378.

14 Lodi-Smith, J., & Roberts, B. W. (2007). Social investment and personality: A meta-analysis of the relationship of personality traits to investment in work, family, religion, and volunteerism. *Personality and Social Psychology Review*, 11(1), 68–86.

15 Ozer, D.J., & Benet-Martínez, V. (2006). Personality and the prediction of consequential outcomes. *Annual Review of Psychology*, 57, 401–421.

16 Caspi, A., Roberts, B.W., & Shiner, R.L. (2005). Personality development: Stability and change. *Annual Review of Psychology*, 56: 453–484.

17 Brent Donnellan M. & Richard W. Robins (2010). Resilient, Overcontrolled, and Undercontrolled Personality Types: Issues and Controversies, 4(11), 1070–1083.

18 Bateman T.S., & Crant J.M. (1993). The proactive component of organizational behavior: A measure and correlates. *Journal of Organizational Behavior*, 14(2), 103–118.

19 Maurer, T.J., & Chapman, E.F. (2018). Relationship of proactive personality with life satisfaction during late career and early retirement. *Journal of Career Development*, 45(4), 345–360.

20 Schiavon, Cecilia C., Marchetti, Eduarda, Gurgel, Léia G., Busnello, Fernanda M., & Reppold, Caroline T. (2017). Optimism and hope in chronic disease: A systematic review. *Frontiers in Psychology*, 7.

21 Lee, L.O., James, P., Zevon, E.S., Kim, E.S., Trudel-Fitzgerald, C., Spiro, A. 3rd, Grodstein, F., & Kubzansky, L.D. (2019). Optimism is associated with exceptional longevity in 2 epidemiologic cohorts of

men and women. *Proceedings of the National Academy of Sciences of the United States of America*, 116(37), 18357–18362.

22 Rozanski, A., Bavishi, C., Kubzansky, L.D., & Cohen, R. (2019). Association of optimism with cardiovascular events and all-cause mortality: A systematic review and meta-analysis. *JAMA Network Open*, 2(9), e1912200.

23 Levy, B. (2022) *Breaking the Age Code*. Ebury.

24 Seligman M. (2011). *Flourish*. Nicholas Brealey Publishing.

25 Hansson, I., Buratti, S., Johansson, B., & Berg, A.I. (2018). Beyond health and economy: Resource interactions in retirement adjustment. *Aging and Mental Health*, 23(11), 1546–1554.

26 Bandura, A. (1997). *Self-Efficacy: The Exercise of Control*. Worth Publishers.

27 Topa, G., & Valero, E. (2017). Preparing for retirement: How self-efficacy and resource threats contribute to retirees' satisfaction, depression, and losses, *European Journal of Work and Organizational Psychology*.

28 Skaalvik, E. M., & Skaalvik, S. (2010). Teacher self-efficacy and teacher burnout: A study of relations. *Teaching and Teacher Education*, 26(4), 1059–1069.

29 Gernigon, C., & Delloye, J.B. (2003). Self-efficacy, causal attribution, and track athletic performance following unexpected success or failure among elite sprinters. *The Sport*.

30 Kim, J.E. & Moen, P. (2002). Retirement transitions, gender, and psychological well-being: A life-course, ecological model. *Journals of Gerontology: Psychological Sciences*, 57B, 212–222.

31 Pearlin, L., & Schooler, C. (1978). The structure of coping. *Journal of Health and Social Behavior*, 19, 2–21.

32 Lachman, M.E., & Burack, O.R. (1993). Planning and control processes across the life span: An overview. *International Journal of Behavioral Development*, 16, 131–143.

33 Rokeach, M. (1973). *The Nature of Human Values*. Free Press, New York.

34 Roccas, S., Sagiv, L., Schwartz, S. H., & Knafo, A. (2002). The big five personality factors and personal values. *Personality and Social Psychology Bulletin*, 28, 789–801.

35 Gouveia, V.V., Vione, K.C., Milfont, T.L., & Fischer, R. (2015). Patterns of value change during the life span: Some evidence from a functional approach to values. *Personality and Social Psychology Bulletin*, 41(9), 1276–1290.

36 Hansson et al., Beyond health and economy.

37 Oreg, S., ayazit, M., Vakola, M., Arciniega, L., Armenakis, A., Barkauskiene, R., Bozionelos, N., Fujimoto, Y., Fernández, L., Han, J., Hrebícková, M., Jimmieson, N., Kordacová, J., Mitsuhashi, H., Mlacic, B., Feric, I., Topic, M., Ohly, S., Saksvik, P., & van Dam, K., (2008). Dispositional resistance to change: Measurement equivalence and

the link to personal values across 17 nations. *The Journal of Applied Psychology*, 93, 935–944.

38 Burr et al., Affective well-being in retirement.

39 Henning, G., Stenling, A., Tafvelin, S., Hansson, I., Kivi, M., Johansson, B., & Lindwall, M. (2019). Preretirement work motivation and subsequent retirement adjustment: A self-determination theory perspective. *Work, Aging and Retirement*, 5(2), 189–203.

40 Houlfort, N., Fernet, C., & Vallerand R. (2015). The role of passion for work and need satisfaction in psychological adjustment to retirement. *Journal of Vocational Behavior*, 88, 84–94.

41 Tajfel, H. (1978). Social categorization, social identity, and social comparison. In H. Tajfel (Ed.), *Differentiation Between Social Groups: Studies in the Social Psychology of Intergroup Relations* (61–76). London: Academic Press.

42 Michinov, E., Fouquereau, E., & Fernandez, A. (2008). Retirees' Social Identity and satisfaction with retirement. *The International Journal of Aging and Human Development*, 66(3), 175–194.

43 Ibid.

44 Ibid.

45 Jetten, J., Haslam, C., Haslam, S.A., Dingle, G., & Jones, J.M. (2014). How groups affect our health and well-being: The path from theory to policy. *Social Issues and Policy Review*, 8, 103–130.

PART 2

REVIEW

Key aspects of your retirement life

WHY WE WORK, AND FILLING THE GAP

Why you should read this chapter

Money is clearly one of the reasons for us to work, but work is far more important than that. Alongside a source of income, work gives us a life routine, a structured use of time, a source of personal status and identity, a context for social interaction, and a meaningful experience that can provide a sense of accomplishment.[1] Whilst we could continue in our current work, as we consider retirement, we have many options, from changing career, reducing hours, or a greater focus on volunteering and leisure activity. We can focus on learning and development or find a passionate interest that takes up much of our time; whether or not it is paid could be less important. All options are considered in this chapter. Have your journal ready and take your time as you work through the activities; this will help you focus, both for now and in the longer term.

TAKE A BREAK

After leaving our full-time work, most of us need a break, time to step away from the pressure of the job. This can be seen as a sabbatical, a good time to recharge and reflect on life moving forward, time to consider our future and to enjoy an extended holiday. Whether you already have some ideas for what to do or are open to considering options, this chapter is for you … and if you truly don't want to think about it, you can come back when the time is right.

DOI: 10.4324/9781003374206-7

During this sabbatical period, if it is more than six months, there could be a downside if you want to return to similar work; you can lose touch with business trends and lose touch with your business contacts. If you plan to go back to work, it is worth creating a return-to-work plan, as someone may do after taking a career break for caring duties, to bring yourself up to date. Equally, if you plan to move to something new, you can do courses, undertake shadowing, and volunteer to increase your understanding of the new type of work.

Moving to a life after full-time work can lead to a loss of status, and the more successful you are, the more difficult it can be to transition to something new, as you don't want to give up this success. People can also, potentially, lose the meaning and purpose that has been gained from their work.[2,3] In the transition phase of retirement there is often excitement over how to fill our days, with time for hobbies, interests, and travels.[4] However, for some people this is not enough, when work has provided them with a meaningful experience; there is a gap to be filled. Many retired people report feeling a sense of emptiness and loss of meaning in this phase of life.[5] Being busy is not enough; indeed, it can stop a person taking up the challenge to find meaning. We will focus on meaning in Part 3.

OPTIONS

The traditional view of retirement was often based on the male perspective, as 50 years ago fewer women had careers; with more women of my generation approaching retirement, we have differing ideas, as do men! There is no longer one dominant pattern of retirement; in its place is "a diverse mix of pathways shaped by occupational identities, finances, health, and perceptions of retirement".[6] However, the design of personal retirement plans can still be impacted by various factors such as life events, cultural norms, workplace and governmental policies, and societal expectations and these may not align with evolving perspectives on what constitutes a fulfilling and prosperous retirement.

As we reach our 60s and begin to think of retirement, it can mean different things to different people. We live longer, healthier lives, and this is added to the middle of our life, not the end, so many want to continue with active, engaged lives for longer. Some people will prefer the traditional clean-break model of retirement, where they stop work completely and transition to a distinct period of leisure in later life. Others will still see retirement as a distinct and desirable phase of life and will continue to engage in a range of work activities, albeit at a potentially reduced scale that provides them with structure and purpose. This can be a move to part-time or flexible working or time to pursue an encore career where people take on a 'person-driven job' with a focus on meaning and social impact,[7] or look for a way of spending our time beyond paid work. More and more people intend to work into retirement, often part-time, and this can include unpaid work – both volunteering and caring duties. A survey from Merrill Lynch and Age Wave said that over 60 per cent want to work to stay mentally active and 46 per cent to remain physically active.

A third option is to stop seeing retirement as a distinct phase and this is where I see the future for many of those who follow us. People will move in and out of work and as they return to study, care for children, care for their parents, take a sabbatical, and continue with this pattern until they reach old-old age and are unable to continue.

Sometimes we can feel forced into retirement; there is some subtle pressure from our colleagues and manager. Barry was told by his younger workmates that he was too old for the job and noticed that people around his age were leaving. Lyn felt she had no option, as she had to take on caring duties for both her mother and husband. Margaret was feeling burned out, but with a final salary pension she was in a fortunate position and chose to stop work and instead focused on her interests.

The age of 66 should not be the end of our time of contribution, but contribution can be broader than continuing to work, even though the UK government want people to remain in the workforce. After full-time work, many people remain socially productive members of society, even though they may not be financially productive. They may not be in paid work, but undertake caring responsibility and volunteering. It can be argued that this is important 'work' and has been included in definitions of productive activity.[8,9]

When I've run pre-retirement seminars, most delegates were not interested in considering this area and preferred to think of the holidays, the grandchildren, the updating their home and garden, but whilst these fill the time, they don't fulfil the full breadth of what we miss from work. It was always satisfying to have people contact me a couple of years on, feeling lost and adrift and ready to consider work and the alternatives, wishing they had explored it earlier.

As we consider our options it is worth thinking about what sort of routine will be right for you. To what extent is identity important to you? What gives you meaning and a sense of accomplishment? How will you live in line with your values? What will give you space to develop and grow? But let's start by looking back on your working life and how satisfied you were with it.

WORK

Some people love their job, and they can't imagine life without working. They may have few other interests or hobbies; they live and breathe their work. It can be hard when it is time to stop working; in fact, many never do. They continue with their job with little thought to what else they could have done, and, too late, they realise they have missed out.

Some stay in work because they are workaholics, and work is their addiction. As these individuals finish tasks, respond to emails, produce reports, or receive recognition from their managers for a job well done, their brains release neurotransmitters such as serotonin and dopamine, which induce feelings of happiness. When they are not working, they may experience a craving for this positive feeling, which motivates them to keep working. Additionally, accomplishing goals can create a sense of internal pride, leading to similar bursts of happy chemicals in the brain.

For others, like Simon, it was a means to an end, and he couldn't wait to retire. He had some plans and ideas, but they didn't quite work out and he drifted for several years. Many of my clients were looking forward to something new. Some took on a new career/job where money was secondary; with a pension they could do what they loved. Others, like Henry, focused more on their voluntary activities and interests. And me … at 61, I started studying for my doctorate and trained as a Vision Quest guide – neither bringing in money, but the satisfaction of learning was draw enough.

Whether you are looking for paid work, voluntary work, or a new and absorbing hobby, it will help to review your career history. But first, what do you gain from working?

Looking back at your career and work history

You may have been in the same profession for years, or already changed career paths a few times. As we ponder whether to include some paid work as we move ahead in life, it is worth taking some time to consider our career story.

Activity 5.1

First, list your different jobs in chronological order and make a note of the tasks each job covered. You can then list the skills relevant to each job. Either use your journal or create a document online.

As you consider each job, think about the things that you did – which of them made you feel energised? You want to have more of this and less of the things that drained you.

Job title and date	Tasks and skills	Key achievements	What energised me

Activity 5.2

Going deep could be a separate book in itself, so let me pose some questions to get you thinking. I'd like you to look back at your recent career history and answer these questions to help you to see the positive and negatives from your work.

	Disagree	Middle view	Agree
I feel fulfilled by my work.			
My job uses my skills and talents; I want to continue to use them.			
I am not under undue stress through my work.			
My work is in line with my values.			
My work gives me time to pursue my hobbies and interests.			
I see my work as a calling, and I would do this work even if the pay was greatly reduced.			
My work allows me scope to mentor and support a younger generation.			
My work is creative and inspiring.			
I enjoy the variety in my day-to-day life.			
My job allows me to learn new things.			
I am stimulated by the people I meet in my working life.			
I am respected for the work I do.			
I gain meaning through my work – it gives me a sense of purpose.			
I am well paid for the work I do.			
I work with people I consider friends.			
The work I do is valued by others.			
I am energised by my work.			
I have the flexibility to work the hours I want and at the location of my choice.			
I enjoy the challenge and want to continue being challenged through my work.			
I enjoy managing other people.			
I have an opportunity to mentor others.			
I have balance in my work and wider life.			
My work gives me a structure to my day and week.			

Review your answers to the above questions; there may be a pattern to where you score most high or low, so consider your answers and make a note in your journal, particularly of what you want more of and less of in your life ahead. You may like to discuss this with your reflections buddy.

Activity 5.3

Let's now return to earlier times. Think back to when you were a child, at 5, 10, and 15. What were you passionate about, what did you dream of doing, what ideas did you discard in pursuit of the sensible option? If there is something bubbling under that you would still love to do, you want to get it out there to consider if it is still possible to pursue, in some form. Make a note of your unfulfilled dreams in your journal. It can be hard to open up to this part of our past, so take yourself out of your head by allowing thoughts to come as you walk out in nature and be open to what you recall.

Did you dream of writing a novel? Why not take a creative writing course. Have a love of steam trains? Be like George and volunteer with the local steam railway and become a travelling ticket inspector. Wanted to be a dancer? Then start taking classes. Write it down in your journal and share your ideas with your reflections buddy.

Activity 5.4

You have just looked back on your life. Now let's look forward. What would you love to learn? Are there skills you would like to develop? Take some time to consider this and make a note in your diary. This can be both things related to work or broader areas.

You have spent time looking at yourself in the last chapter and considering yourself at work in this chapter. Let's now summarise what you are looking for, which could be via paid work, volunteering, or an absorbing hobby. You can carry on with using nature as a guide as you complete this activity.

Activity 5.5

You may like to imagine that you are a plant at a garden centre. Describe the sort of environment where you will thrive and how much attention you need to grow. This is far richer than a bullet-point list and helps get you ready for the next chapter in your life. Summarise this in a statement and write it down in your journal. You may also like to share this more widely and get some feedback from others. It's an interesting activity and it might inspire others to do it too.

GENERATIVITY

You may have come across Erikson's eight stages of psychosocial development.[10] This begins at birth with trust vs. mistrust and comes under the virtue of hope. Around our age (40 to 65) we reach generativity vs. stagnation with a basic virtue of care, before moving on to the wisdom virtue (ego integrity vs. despair). If we don't keep 'generating' value, engaging with the world, and pushing our careers forward, we are doomed to 'stagnate' as inertia and complacency overtake us. Generativity is an integral component of the healthy adult personality. The generative adult maintains a concern for the well-being of younger and future generations. Their actions promote the growth of specific younger individuals and establish a favourable environment in which all persons may develop to achieve their fullest potential.

If we are feeling bored or under-appreciated in our job, it is likely because we are not aligned with the generativity and caring tendencies of this age stage. Let's consider some ways you can move towards generativity. It could be to volunteer; is there a cause or organisation that you feel connected to? It may be to be a mentor (which is not telling people what to do but supporting them to find their own way); this could be in your workplace or it could be with a younger person you know or through a voluntary organisation; perhaps to be of support to a young person who has moved from fostering to living alone.

Being more open to the people we meet, and listening more, can identify informal opportunities to do this. By building relationships with younger people, it can also lead to 'reverse mentoring'. Younger people can think differently and open our eyes to the new.

I've introduced generativity here as so many of the people I work with raise the question of 'Is this it?' and want to focus more on giving back and doing something more useful and meaningful in their lives; this is an important stage in our development. In my research, generativity was a predictor of job satisfaction and attitudes towards retirement. We will be coming back to this in Chapter 9.

Activity 5.6

As we review our lives, we become more aware of what we are grateful for and writing it down, on a regular basis, is a good habit to start. We looked at having a gratitude journal in Chapter 4.

Make a note of the ways that you make a difference to others. It could be an offer of help, giving your full attention to someone as they talk, or standing up for those in need. Write it down in your journal and continue to add as you become aware of things you have done and the actions you take in the future.

This chapter will continue with career options before looking at the alternatives – volunteering, study, and a focus on a passionate interest. Whichever you choose, you will want to ensure you can use your strengths and feel in flow.

Flow

Flow is a state of mind where you become fully immersed in an activity, feeling completely absorbed and focused on the present moment. The concept of flow was first introduced by psychologist Mihály Csíkszentmihályi,[11] who described it as a state of optimal experience. When in flow, people often lose track of time and are fully engaged in the activity they are performing. Flow can occur during any type of activity, from work and creative pursuits to sports and hobbies. It is characterised by a feeling of energised focus, a sense of control, and a deep enjoyment of the task at hand. Flow has been associated with increased productivity, creativity, and overall well-being.

CHANGING CAREER

What we want from a job can vary over time. Earlier in our career, it is often about gaining a reputation, getting promoted, and salary increase. Later in life it is more about levels of satisfaction and often about how we can support the next generation; to step up to the role of elder. As our 60s can be a time to reflect on our career, it may be that you want a change of career, either to an encore career or to re-career. People will continue with work for different reasons: social reasons to interact with others; personal reasons to include self-esteem, self-efficacy, personal satisfaction, and a sense of pride; financial reasons, such as income and other benefits; and a need to teach and share knowledge with a younger generation (generative reasons).[12]

We will look at health in the next chapter, but it is worth saying here that sometimes we are driven to bridge employment and a change of career because of health issues. For some, manual jobs can become too much with bad backs, arthritis, and possibly heart problems. If you are unable to see yourself in your job at state retirement age, it is often a reason to change career sooner.

A health condition that limits an ability to work increases the likelihood of moving to self-employment as it can be easier to support accommodations required for health reasons when you are in charge of your own career. Those who felt they would not be able to work past the age of 62 were more likely to re-career to self-employment after age 50.[13]

False retirements and return to work

After a couple of years of full-on retirement, many want to return to work. This first retirement can be seen as a sabbatical to recharge and review life going forward. Taking a break gives us time to reassess what's important to us. People return to work for different reasons. For some it is financial reasons (37%), for others because they are bored (35%). With Covid, and Brexit, there is more need for older workers, but there remain barriers to a return to work. Whilst some employers are open to the talent that we can bring, many recruiters hold ageist views and we can be seen as over-qualified and so are forced to remove some of our qualifications.

THE FOUR TYPES OF WORKING RETIREES

While some work primarily for the money, many others are motivated by important non-financial reasons such as staying mentally and physically active, maintaining social connections, and for self-worth.

Some are high-achievers and could be seen as workaholics. Work is their life. At the other extreme are those who are working to pay the bills. It is a need for income that drives them. In between are those who are focused on supporting a cause or giving back and can be found working in the not-for-profit sector, and it could be voluntary work; they are not driven by money. The last group are those who seek balance; some part-time work alongside their wider interests. They work for fun and connection.

If we do return to work, we need to think about where we fit in the organisational structure. Would you be happy to be closer to the bottom than the top and to work for someone much younger, and probably less experienced than yourself? It can be hard to stop ourself from giving advice and trying to solve a problem and, if we do, it can make a less experienced manager feel insecure.

Some of us are not making decisions on salary alone. For others, income generation is essential, and will lead on choices made. If you want or need to work, you have choices: a return to what you did before, part-time consultancy, bridge employment, a new career, self-employment, or a portfolio career.

1. Part-time working for your current employer

As you consider retirement, you can talk to your current employer about moving to working on a part-time basis; this can be useful for both you and your organisation, as it retains knowledge within the organisation and can also help to maintain our well-being and overall life satisfaction.

2. Work as a consultant

If you have relevant skills and experience and connections, you may be able to get lucrative work as a consultant. This work is uncertain, and consultants often talk of feast or famine but if you have a pension and don't need the money for bills it can be a nice side earner.

3. Bridge employment

Bridge employment is often seen as a less stressful and demanding job, often part-time or of short duration.[14] It can include working as a teaching assistant or in a call centre. McDonalds had a campaign to target older workers who are 'not the retiring type' and many people work at B&Q, Starbucks, Tesco, etc. There is nothing wrong with these organisations, but if you seek meaningful work, you may want to see these organisations as a bridge while you decide what you really want to do, and if you are stuck or unsure, coaching will be of great benefit.

There are benefits to organisations that recruit an older worker in a mainly young workforce. McDonalds data has found that an older worker calms the whole place down and allows it to run much more efficiently; there is less competition, and younger workers have someone they can turn to for advice.

4. Something new, including creating a business

Others opt for re-careering, which is when people make a decision to embark on a new career or a move of industry after a long time working in one career.[15] It is a change of work without being seen as a bridge to retirement and may be something you considered or chose to do in your 50s, as one big change before retirement looms closer. It could include a move to self-employment and a decision to view career success in a different way to earlier in your career. Something new can involve retraining and a return to study, so it is worth considering in advance of retirement so that you can start gaining new skills or undertake short courses to get things in place.

Many people seek a life of greater meaning, and this includes their work; they want to make a significant contribution to wider society. They hope to find their calling. This can include working in education, health care, local government, and the not-for-profit sector. This move is as significant as any move when younger and needs to be well-researched with an adapted CV and LinkedIn profile, with good use made of connecting with people.

Is a calling important to you?

Work can be seen as a job, a career, or a calling. Calling refers to the focus on activities that are significant at the moral, social, and personal levels.[16] A person with a calling is not driven by income or career progression but from the fulfilment gained from their work.[17] You may have a job that is considered a calling and seen as such by others, such as a teacher, nurse, or artist; but maybe not. Moving forward, you may now want to follow a calling. For too long, you did a job that you felt you had to do; now you can do what you want and we can certainly have a calling in retirement.

Activity 5.7

Would you say that you have a calling for a particular type of work? Are you trying to decide what your calling is or is this of no relevance to you?

You may already feel called to do something, but, if not, you may like to think in what way you may like to help others or if there is something else that may give you meaning. Volunteering is just one option to consider.

Creating a business is a dream of many and needs to be carefully considered before putting your life savings into a venture.

It can include some false starts and challenges, and it is better to go in with 'eyes open' than to believe the stories popular in the press. Too many articles in the media make it look easy – moving to the seaside to set up a B&B, or a tea shop in a quaint touristy town – with little coverage of the many who don't make it a success.

5. Self-employment

People often choose self-employment because they want more autonomy and flexibility, but it can also be because they have found it difficult to continue in salaried work due to age discrimination or to manage health challenges. When someone has experienced ageism in their workplace, they may decide this is their only option. With less certainty of income, it is often the choice of those who are financially secure. For some, the work is related to a hobby, such as jewellery-making or motorcycle maintenance, and for others they can continue in their career as a consultant. It can also include being a self-employed delivery driver. A side-hustle can be a way to build something to continue with well beyond a traditional retirement age.

6. Portfolio career

Charles Handy coined the phrase 'portfolio career' and described it as a collection of 'bits and pieces of work', seeing life as a collection of groups and activities.[18] As we head towards retirement, we can step into a new area through a portfolio career, made up of both paid and unpaid activities. This will often be created by a move from full-time to part-time working, giving space to start something new.

The benefit of a portfolio career is that there is no need for a clear retirement; people can gradually move to less work as they adjust their workload and responsibilities in line with life demands. Depending on your skills and experience it can lead to well-paid part-time opportunities, working as, for example, a finance director for two or more smaller companies who get the benefit of your experience for a much-lower financial outlay, or one paid job, some study, and some voluntary activity. Mike continues using his accountancy skills as a self-employed bookkeeper alongside regular volunteering in a charity shop, his hobby of model railways, and time 'to be', walking in nature.

Activity 5.8

Any thoughts for what you want to do next? Make a note in your journal.

CHOOSING A NEW CAREER

If you want a different type of career or to try out some different work, these six steps will help you to identify options:

1. Understand yourself

Using what you found out about yourself in the last chapter and earlier in this chapter, make sure you are clear on your personality, values, skills, and abilities. Be clear on what energises you and, also, the sort of people that energise you. Is there a cause that really excites you? It could be the environment, young or old people, transport … from an interest in a cause you can then see potential work related to it. Also, consider what you liked and disliked from each job you had, and your reason for leaving.

2. Identity options

What would you love to do? What comes easily based on your career history? You can research online to find out more and dig deeper through talking with people. Working in finance can be very different in a small family business to a large multinational and working in manufacturing is different to an arts organisation. It can help to start an ideas file; as you read books, browse online, read the newspaper, or see a job on a TV show, you are likely to get ideas. List them and keep articles in a folder ready to review.

3. What's important to you?

Is it flexibility, location, learning, ease of entry, something new? Make a note on a spreadsheet of possible careers/jobs/options down the left-hand side and criteria that is important to you across the top row. You can then compare your options against each other, giving them a rating on a 1 to 5 scale.

4. Decision-making through switching off

Whilst you can decide logically based on the ratings in the grid suggested above, you can also allow your brain some space by getting out into nature. When we are not focused on decision-making, we can often make our best decisions.

5. Check out your decision

Do you need to do more research? Have you spoken to people who work in the industry or the job; have you done some short courses, for example, in climate change or historical writing? If you are thinking about your own business, have a look at what other people offer and their process and think about how you would compete. Would it help to do some voluntary work first to test it out? Or it could be that voluntary work would give you enough freedom and flexibility.

6. Connecting with others

We look at wider relationships in Chapter 7, but we also need to consider connecting with others as we think about work. Many times, we find out about opportunities for work through the people we know, and these are often gained through our work connections. Once we leave our job, it can be harder to maintain these and so people seek out new networks, which can include family and friends, through interest groups, and reconnecting with university networks and previous work colleagues on LinkedIn. Particularly when we choose a self-employed route, we need to create new networks, not only to find opportunities but also for support when things get tough, and to bounce around ideas. Pay attention to connections with people from a different generation to you; it may well be that someone of that age group interviews you for a job and they may know about opportunities and trends that your contemporaries are less aware of.

FILLING THE GAP – VOLUNTEERING

If money isn't a key driver, volunteering may fill the gap from work. Volunteering can also help us to develop the skills needed for a change of career and build our confidence before a return to a paid job. There are many organisations which only exist through their network of supporters. It can also be a time to 'give back' and make a meaningful contribution to society.[19]

Volunteering can include more involvement with the local community, such as becoming a parish councillor or school governor, or to campaign for a cause. As I write this book, I've moved home and I'm now within walking distance of a nature-focused art gallery where I plan to volunteer later this year. You get the same physical and mental benefits as in paid work, and it can also help you to live longer. According to research,[20] this is true if you are volunteering to help others; interestingly, the research found that it didn't have the same impact when people were doing it for more selfish reasons.

There are both personal and wider benefits to voluntary working, such as expressing values, social benefits, career benefits, escaping negative feelings, learning, increasing levels of self-esteem and self-efficacy,[21] life satisfaction,[22] and enhanced integration with communities.[23] Research identified that people volunteer to help others (83%), to feel useful and productive (65%), and 'to fulfil a moral responsibility' (51%).

Another research study found that an older volunteer is more likely to prefer a people-orientated role, with more responsibility rather than admin. They want regular training and information-sharing to increase levels of competence and so have less need for supervision – worth bearing in mind as you consider options.

It's certainly worth keeping your options open and trying out a few organisations so you can see how you fit in. Carol found that the people at a historical house were overly demanding, whereas the local theatre was a delight and she got to watch films and plays for free, too. Carol had volunteered prior to her retirement, and so continued. Research has found that when people haven't volunteered whilst in work, they are less likely to volunteer in retirement, but you could well be the exception.

FILLING THE GAP – LONG-LIFE LEARNING, HOBBIES, AND INTERESTS

Our lives are far more than our job and career, but too many people allow work to expand and take over their life. Do you have some hobbies and interests? It's worth making a note below of what you do have. Our interests can include going to watch a sports game or to the theatre, time spent playing computer games or listening to music. Are you happy with the time spent on these interests? Is there something you would love to do, and you can focus more on, in this next stage of life?

Activity 5.9

My hobby or interest	How frequently I pursue it	How much time I would ideally like to spend on it	Other comments

Activity 5.10

You may also like to consider what activities challenge your thinking? Do you read about ideas, gather new information, solve problems, and try out new ideas? If not, is this something you would like to do? Maybe start with puzzles such as Sudoku or quizzes. I'd like you to journal about this and to identify at least three new ideas to pursue.

What we do next does not need to revolve around earning money. We may finally have the time to spend on what is of great interest to us. For Helen, it was to devote more time to historical research; for Arthur, his photography; and for David and Mary, to devote more time to nature through the purchase of a wood.

If you dream of taking up watercolour painting or learning a language, you could start now, and have a test go rather than wait. I had a client who planned to take up bowls on retirement, ignored my suggestion to start whilst in work, and when the time came, he found it wasn't as interesting as he thought. A new interest could include getting involved with a social movement, for example, to campaign against climate change.

Research has found that social hobbies are more likely to lead to happiness and that people who engage in three or four different activities are happier than those who engage in just one or two. It also found that people may experience psychological barriers to the enjoyment of leisure if they lack a clear definition of value for leisure activities, have not learned enjoyable leisure earlier in life, and lack hobbies or preferences for use of their free time.[24]

If you need inspiration, I've got a massive list (317!) on my website – https://denisetaylor.co.uk/rethinking-retirement/ – which ranges from aerobics, antiques, and astrology to weaving, writing poetry, and yoga.

Appreciation For nature

Many of us work inside and have hobbies and interests that involve technology. Our mental health is improved by being outside, so if you live in an urban area, you may want to check you are spending enough time in the natural environment where you can listen to the wind and the birds and look out at wonderful scenery. It's a great place to unplug from the technological world. As we age, we are likely to spend more time in the natural world, and this could be walking, birdwatching, volunteering, or to focus more on forest bathing.

LONG-LIFE LEARNING

Remaining curious keeps us young and builds our confidence. It can open us to new opportunities. There are so many options, from short online courses and the wide number of MOOCs (massive open online courses), joining U3A (University of the Third Age) or Oddfellows to going back to university for academic studies. It could help with gaining work opportunities or it could be purely for its own sake. If you always wanted to study French literature or learn motorcycle maintenance, why not do a course now? I've been reading of a woman, now over 90, who seemed to be addicted to learning, with four master's degrees and now studying for a PhD. If you want the academic qualification, why not? But learning doesn't have to be formal.

Many of us never got a chance to go to university, leaving to start work at 16 and learning on the job, or perhaps a part-time degree later, but with a focus on our career. Forced to leave school myself at 15, I started to study with the Open University in my early 20s and continued to study; I became an effective learner, learning short cuts. Only later did I realise I had missed out on all the non-essential reading. One of the joys of academic study in my 60s was to have more time, and at one point I went down a side avenue and spent three weeks looking into the meaning of meaning which ended up as one paragraph in my thesis, but I was so glad I fully explored the philosophy of meaning.

Learning does not need to be academic, and it could lead to some paid work – sewing, cooking, computer programming, or web design. It could be related to activities such as learning martial arts or to dance. It may be related to personal development – gaining the confidence to undertake public speaking, learning a foreign language so you can read *Les Misérables* or *À la recherche du temps perdu* (*In Search of Lost Time*) in the original French, or you may want to become a better listener.

Seamus decided to learn Irish and found a course via Future Learn. He also realised he could benefit from learning computer skills, so with a new computer and YouTube videos he is becoming more proficient. He still plans to learn more about photography, but for that wants a face-to-face course rather than to learn anything else on line.

Vidhi started to learn Lindy Hop and found a social life through regular attendance at classes. She then moved on to Burlesque classes – not to perform on stage but to give her more self-confidence. I've also done Burlesque classes and it was great fun.

Activity 5.11

Make a note of anything you would like to learn, or to be able to do. Also make a note of what motivates you. Understanding your motivation will give clarity on your likelihood of success. For example, with an interest of history, do you want to know more about where you live or do you want to go deep into original research as you study for a PhD or MPhil?

BEFORE YOU MOVE ON ...

We've looked at work and its alternatives. Do you now have a plan, or at least some ideas for the short and longer term? Research can help us understand the highs and lows of any option we consider, and trying things out via shadowing, volunteering, or a short course will be helpful. We want to get things right and there is less time ahead for wrong turns. Alongside more traditional online learning, you can find many useful videos via YouTube and TikTok.

We are likely to need people to support us, to be clear on our financial position, and also to consider options should we have a health setback. James had not expected to need a triple bypass, and this led to changes in his work plans. We will move on to health and well-being in the next chapter.

NOTES

1 Friedmann, E.A., & Havighurst, R.J. (1954). *The Meaning of Work and Retirement*. The University of Chicago Press.

2 Reis, M., & Gold, D.P. (1993). Retirement, personality, and life satisfaction: A review and two models. *The Journal of Applied Gerontology*, 12, 261–282.

3 Wang, M., & Shi, J. (2014). Psychological research on retirement. *Annual Review of Psychology*, 65, 209–233.

4 Osbourne J.W., (2009). Commentary on retirement, identity, and Erikson's developmental stage model. *Canadian Journal on Aging / La Revue canadienne du vieillissement*, 28(04), 295–301.

5 Jonsson, H., Borell, L., & Sadlo, G. (2000). Retirement: An occupational transition with consequences for temporality, balance and meaning of occupations, *Journal of Occupational Science*, 7(1), 29–37.

6 Kojola, E., & Moen, P. (2016). No more lock-step retirement: Boomers' shifting meanings of work and retirement. *Journal of Aging Studies*, 36, 59–70.

7 Freedman, M. (2007). *Encore: Finding Work that Matters in the Second Half of Life*. Perseus, Fredrickson, Cambridge, MA.

8 Goldschmidt-Clermont, L., & Pagnossin-Aligisakis, E. (1995). *Measures of Unrecorded Economic Activities in Fourteen Countries*. Human Development Report Office, New York.

9 Herzog, A.R., & Morgan, J.N. (1992). Age and gender differences in the value of productive activities: Four different approaches. *Research on Aging*, 14(2), 169–198.

10 Erikson, E. H. (1963). *Childhood and Society* (2nd ed.). Norton, New York.

11 Csíkszentmihályi, M. (1990). *Flow: The Psychology of Optimal Experience*. Harper, New York.

12 Dendinger, V. M., Adams, G.A., & Jacobson, J. D. (2005). Reasons for working and their relationship to retirement attitudes, job satisfaction and occupational self-efficacy of bridge employees. *International Journal of Ageing & Human Development*, 61(1), 21–35.

13 Zissimopoulos, J. M., & Karoly, L. A. (2007). Transitions to self-employment at older ages: The role of wealth, health, health insurance and other factors. *Labour Economics*, 14(2), 269–295.

14 Cahill, K.E., Giandrea, M.D., & Quinn, J.F. (2006). Retirement patterns from career employment. *The Gerontologist*, 46(4), 514–552.

15 Johnson, R., J, K., & Lewis, E. (2009). Older workers on the move: Recareering in later life. *AARP Public Policy Institute, April.*

16 Wrzesniewski, A., Dekas, K., & Rosso, B. (2009). Calling. In S. J. Lopez & A. Beauchamp (Eds.), *The Encyclopaedia of Positive Psychology* (115–118). Blackwell Publishing.

17 Wrzesniewski, A., McCauley, C., Rozin, P., & Schwartz, B. (1997). Jobs, careers, and callings: People's relations to their work. *Journal of Research in Personality*, 31(1), 21–33.

18 Handy, C. (2002). *The Empty Raincoat*. Arrow Books.

19 Sargent, L.D., Lee, M.D., Martin, B., & Zikic, J. (2013). Reinventing retirement: New pathways, new arrangements, new meanings. *Human Relations*, 1, 3–21.

20 Konrath, Sara, Fuhrel-Forbis, Andrea, Lou, Alina, & Brown, Stephanie. (2012). Motives for Volunteering Are Associated with Mortality Risk in Older Adults. Health Psychology, 31(1), 87–96.

21 Morrow-Howell, N., Hong, S.I., & Tang, F. (2009). Who benefits from volunteering? Variations in perceived benefits. *The Gerontologist,* 49(1), 91–102.

22 Moen, P., & Fields, V. (2002). Midcourse in the United States: Does unpaid community participation replace paid work? *Ageing International*, 27, 21–48.

23 Stukas A., Daly M., & Cowling M., (2005) Volunteerism and social capital: a functional approach. *Australian Journal on Volunteering,* 10(2), 35–44.

24 Myers, D.G. (1999). Close relationships and quality of life. In D. Kahneman, E. Diener, & N. Schwarz (Eds.), *Well-being: The Foundations of Hedonic Psychology* (374–391). Russell Sage Foundation.

6

HEALTH AND WELL-BEING

Why you should read this chapter

Health is probably more important than our finances. If we haven't been making it a priority, today is a good day to start to focus on areas to maintain and improve our health and well-being. We can make some minor changes and make big differences in the longer term. I've been reviewing the literature and research to help you make choices for the future and letting you know positive steps you can take. I'll explain the difference between chronological and biological age, and we will be looking at the impact of our attitudes and why we need to be more positive. We will also look at specific things we can do to help us live longer, such as healthy eating, being active, getting enough sleep, stress management, the need for positive relationships, and more.

We all want a long and healthy life, but advancements in healthcare have not led to a decrease in the number of older people in poor health. Currently 59 per cent of UK citizens over the age of 65 have two or more serious health conditions, and this is predicted to reach 70 per cent by 2035. It's unclear how many of these are over 80 but I do know when I visit my dentist or optician, they are often surprised, given my age (65) that I'm not on any medication.

At 65, a man can expect to live another 12.5 years disability free, and a woman, 13.4 years disability free. To increase this period, whatever our approach to health has been so far, now is probably the time to make some changes. Many have

DOI: 10.4324/9781003374206-8

lifestyle diseases and obesity has nearly tripled since 1975; 80 per cent of heart disease, stroke, and type-2 diabetes and 40 per cent of cancer could be prevented, mainly through diet and lifestyle improvements. It's not just about living longer but living longer in good health.

WHAT IS HEALTH?

There is a lot more to health than not being ill. Research is increasingly showing the complex relationships of brain, mind, and body. With many diseases attributable to lifestyle, the main risk factor is our behaviours, and by modifying our behaviour we can significantly reduce the risk of developing these diseases. It's not just physical health; mental health is emerging as a significant global issue and it is anticipated that by 2030, depression will be the biggest single health problem.

A UK government paper[1] identified that well-being comprises two main elements: feeling good and functioning well. Experiencing feelings such as happiness, contentment, enjoyment, curiosity, and engagement are indicative of a positive life experience. Along with these emotional states, our overall well-being is also influenced by our ability to function effectively in the world. This includes having positive relationships, a sense of control over one's life, and a clear sense of purpose. All of these attributes are crucial components of a healthy and fulfilling life.

I'm not a medical doctor, but I have read much on health over the years and wrote the book *Fat to Fantastic*. Although I've put some weight back on, I still weigh 7 stone less than at my biggest. Like you, I want to remain in good health for as long as possible, and I've taken good health for granted. Let's look at the research on retirement and health and see what will help.

RESEARCH ON RETIREMENT AND HEALTH

Research on longevity in 'blue zones' has found that what helps is to have a purpose in life, being curious, having lots of variety, laughter, a sense of belonging, and close connections with friends and family, including shared meals. This is relevant to people of all ages.

Let's now look specifically at research examining the impact of retirement on health and well-being. It leads to a mixed picture. Well-being can improve as people move on from stressful work. For example, Rosenthal and Moore[2] found that if work was stressful and physically straining, retirement can be good for health and a pan-European study found that retirement leads to health improvements for both men and women, and at differing levels of education.[3] Another study[4] found health improved due to less stress, more exercise, and more sleep after retirement, alongside improved mental and physical fatigue and improved depressive symptoms. A systematic review of longitudinal studies[5] found strong evidence for retirement leading to improved mental health which they said could be linked to the loss of work-related stress. Several studies have found the adjustment to be positive, with many beneficial effects to the individuals.[6,7,8]

Yet, despite evidence demonstrating the positive, beneficial effect, retirement is ranked tenth on the list of life's most stressful events.[9] For some, this can be attributable to a reduction in income, sometimes through having to take early retirement.[10] It could also be down to illness after retirement. A study[11] found that there was a 40 per cent increase in having a heart attack or stroke when retired, compared to those still in work. When people have poor health, it can mean a less active retirement, impacting on social interaction and leisure activity. The reduction in the number of social interactions may play a role, with studies suggesting that this can have a negative effect on mental and physical health.[12] People can lose their identity and their social network of work colleagues,[13] and no longer having structure to the day can be detrimental. We also need to consider the difference between forced and chosen retirement. If people have chosen retirement, they are more likely to have found happiness in retirement than if it was forced.[14]

The transition

For most people, retirement is not only a transition between middle and late adulthood (65 and older) but is also associated with important psychological and interpersonal changes that may impact on an individuals' self-esteem and well-being.[15] This is a transition to the later stages of life and an introduction to the realities of ageing, the start of a decline in health and noticing age-related physical and cognitive changes in themselves and others, alongside the mortality of relatives and friends.[16]

Whilst for some, the transition is smooth, up to one third of people who retire find the transition either stressful or notice a decline in their well-being[17] and between 10 and 25 per cent of older workers experience difficulties in adjusting to retirement,[18] In the UK, 25 per cent of retirees experience difficulties which can affect mental health.[19]

We looked at self-employment in the previous chapter; when people had health issues, they would often choose self-employment as an easier way to work. Clearly, some of us will be in poor health, and I have friends who have had to seriously adapt to changing health. Before the pandemic, Alison moved to homeworking to reduce the time spent travelling to work and to have control over her working hours. Kate left work due to stress and burnout and it took over two years before she felt ready to return to work, as she still would slip into depression and anxiety; working as a consultant meant she could tell people she was already booked up when she didn't have the mental strength to work.

CHRONOLOGICAL AND BIOLOGICAL AGE

We know our chronological age, as it is measured from our year of birth to a given date. We also have biological age, also called physiological age and epigenetic age. This is a measure of how well or poorly the body is functioning relative to chronological age, you could be 65 but have a biological age of 40 or 80.

The conventional method of using chronological age to assess one's health, mental capacity, or motivation is no longer relevant. Individuals have more vitality than previous generations did at the same age, and they continue to be productive, mentally sharp, and capable well into their 80s. In fact, a significant portion of people over 85 years old (56%) report having no health-related limitations in performing work or housework, indicating that age should not be a barrier to one's abilities or potential.

Ageing can be accelerated by infections such as HIV, stress (including PTSD), cumulative lifestyle stress, smoking, excess drinking, childhood violence and a high BMI. Some of our genes can be switched on or off by factors such as diet, exercise, psychological approach and attitude. Negative perceptions make it more likely that someone will experience diseases, such as heart disease, suffer heart attacks in later life and die early. We are born with a fixed number of genes or DNA but research by The Irish Longitudinal Study on Ageing (TILDA)[20] found that only 20 per cent of ageing is controlled by our genes, so we can take action to improve our biological clock.

If we feel younger than our chronological age it slows our ageing. We can add over seven years to our life span purely down to our attitudes, so being more positive is an important factor to develop. This is backed up by the Nun Study, a longitudinal study on 678 sisters of School Sisters of Notre Dame who shared a similar lifestyle. They wrote an essay in the 1930s on why they joined the convent. 60 years later, 85 per cent of those who used at least one positive word were still alive.

How long will I live?

There are a number of longevity calculators available online such as this one - https://livingto100.com/calculator, whilst there are things that cannot be accounted for, this can give us a prod to review our health and lifestyle. At some level this is just for fun, but as you answer the questions it can make you decide to modify some behaviours. For example, whilst I floss,

I didn't do it every day, so it was a reminder, other questions made clear on what my source of stress is.

My mum is 90 and still fairly active and optimistic. So that's a good age to aim for. I was truthful on my weight and my results have shown me as living to 97, and if this is in good health for most of the rest of my life, I'll be very happy.

Activity 6.1

You may like to complete this assessment and use it to identify some actions you will take to improve your health. Make a note in your journal and discuss with your reflections buddy. Choose three things you will start today.

Our attitudes

People of the same age can appear and act very differently. In our 80s, someone could be in a care home, someone else still running marathons. A large contribution is down to attitude; Becca Levy's work[21] says that people who have negative attitudes about ageing are likely to die seven and a half years earlier than those with positive attitudes, often because of higher rates of heart disease. Let's look further into this and also more broadly into what can help us have a healthy later life.

Some people are naturally more positive or negative and we can be affected by the people we are with. If they are positive people, with a purpose to life which includes voluntary work and new challenges, you are likely to do the same. If the people are negative and bring you down, you either join them with these attitudes or ideally spend a lot less time in their company.

Research found that older adults with negative attitudes had worse mental abilities compared to participants who were more positive. Negative attitudes towards ageing were associated with a decline in walking speed, worse memory, and poor performance on a number of brain tests. In another study, adults were asked to say how much they agreed with 17 statements such as "I have no control over how getting older affects my social life" and "As I get older, I get wiser." The more these adults agreed with the negative statements and the less they agreed with the positive statements, the worse their attitudes towards ageing, and the more likely they were to experience accelerated physical and cognitive ageing over the following eight years.

How old one feels actually influences how quickly we age. If you feel your chronological age, you are more likely to become frail and have poorer brain health. This is because a positive attitude towards getting older can switch on protective genes which slow the pace of cell ageing. Negative perceptions make diseases such as heart disease more likely and will also increase mortality. A positive attitude towards getting older changes cell chemicals beneficially, possibly by reducing inflammation. Even if we have health problems, our attitude can have a major impact.

Like others who approach life with joy, I don't let my chronological age stop me doing anything. I still feel and act as I did several decades ago, although I recognise that I sometimes need to wait for the blood to return to my feet if I've been sitting for too long. I'm someone who doesn't see age as any reason to hold me back and I maintain an enthusiastic view of life. I recognise my limitations, so don't go for long uphill hikes, but I'm open to new experiences and just before lockdown went to Nepal alone including two days trekking with a local guide.

It's also been found that our attitudes and beliefs can affect the healing process. Expect healing to take a long time and you will probably be proved right, but equally you can assume that healing will be as fast as when younger. If we fall over as an older adult, people refer to it as 'having a fall', and attributed to age, rather than because we were not carefully looking where we are going.

Society attitudes

2022 was the first year I'd heard the term 'OK boomer', and this and others are used as put-downs. There are so many ways society sees ageing in negative terms: from road signs with older people with humped backs and walking sticks, to seeing most older people in adverts advertising funeral plans and joint ointments. We can all be affected by messages, often subtle, and these can raise our stress levels, leading to higher blood pressure and potential health issues and leading to an earlier death. A Yale University study showed how perceptions about ageing can change our physiology. Exposure to positive ideas about ageing – for example, words such as 'sage' – helped participants deal with stress. A barrage of negative stereotypes – for example, 'senile' – increased stress. The World Health Organisation has found little evidence to support the age-related stereotypes found in the media of older people being forgetful, stubborn, and frail.

LIVING LONGER

People will sometimes think that to be healthy and happy they need to be in top physical and mental health, but psychological well-being is not dependent on health. Longevity is correlated with education. This doesn't mean you need a university degree, but it is related to activity that keeps your brain active and to having an open mind and undertaking mental, social, and physical activity.

Dr Perls[22] has said that genetics plays a significant role and accounts for 40 to 50 per cent of those living to 100; however, he also said there is no accurate test to see if we have the longevity gene, so we should save our money if we see one advertised.

Too many people in their 50s talk about their best life being behind them and experiencing lower levels of well-being as they age, but when well-being is assessed across the lifespan, through longitudinal studies, they find a U-shaped graph. At an earlier stage of life our well-being is aligned to accomplishments, as we strive for a better life. In later life, accomplishment is no longer the main source of our well-being, and it is more around positive emotions, connecting with people and a greater sense of meaning.

If we take ourselves back to our earlier years, we can remember how we would look to the future, at what we would achieve. By our mid-50s, we can remember the good times from the past, and this can enhance our well-being. It is not to look back with an overly positive view – most of us have sadness and regrets – but we can see them more as learning experiences, lessons that helped create the person we are today.

There is much in the press about the increase in poor mental health. Mental health improves as we get older as we have better coping mechanisms and become more resilient, with 91 per cent in one study showing high levels of resilience. As we age, we are less bothered by minor hassles and have learned to deal better with stress. We are less likely to get angry and are less emotionally charged compared to younger people. We worry less and experience more positive emotions and less-frequent negative emotions.

This links with what I wrote in Chapter 4 about psychological factors. Optimism is associated with higher levels of physical well-being, and optimists live ten years longer! We also live longer where we have hope, quality relationships, a life of meaning and engagement with the world.

Psychological well-being

We can live longer by following PERMA, which was described by Martin Seligman in his 2011 book, *Flourish*.[23] PERMA stands for: positive emotions, engagement, positive relationships, meaning and purpose, and a sense of accomplishment.

Positive emotions: our overall well-being is closely tied to the presence of positive emotions in our lives, such as happiness, joy, excitement, and contentment. One effective way to increase these positive emotions is by keeping a gratitude diary (see Chapter 4), where you write down three things that went well each day and reflect on why they went well.

Engagement: when we participate in activities that align with our interests and passions, we experience feelings of fulfilment. Such activities – music, sports, hobbies – can lead to the state of 'flow', where one becomes fully immersed in a task and loses a sense of self and time. We discussed flow in Chapter 5.

(Positive) Relationships: maintaining healthy and strong relationships with others is essential for our overall happiness, as they provide us with support, a sense of being valued, and love. More on this in the next chapter.

Meaning and purpose: having a sense of meaning and purpose in daily life is vital for attaining happiness and well-being. Section 3 is focused on this.

A sense of accomplishment: having a sense of purpose and accomplishment is key to our well-being, as it can provide feelings of mastery and achievement and can be linked to what gives us meaning in life.

HEALTHY HABITS

In the book *The 100-Year Life*,[24] Lynda Gratton and Andrew Scott write that we can live longer in one of two ways: living younger for longer, or older for longer. We stand the best chance of living to be healthy and happy at 100 if, alongside the psychological factors above and in Chapter 4, we eat healthily, are active, sleep well, manage stress, have positive relationships, avoid risky substances, and have meaning and purpose to our life.[25]

Let's now take each of these in turn.

1. Eat healthily

There is plenty of evidence on the importance of a more natural-based diet of unprocessed or minimally processed foods with plenty of fruit and vegetables plus nuts, grains, fish, and enough protein. The Mediterranean diet is recommended and can help to lower rates of cardiovascular disease. It is also recommended to eat within an eight-hour window every day, which your body sees as fasting and will switch on protective cell mechanisms beneficial for longevity. There is now a greater understanding of gut microbiome and the need to eat a wide variety of fruits, vegetables, nuts and seeds. I paid to have my gut microbiome measured and, interestingly, my body does not metabolise bread and potatoes as well as rice and pasta; strawberries and cherries are better for me than bananas or blueberries.

Growing up in the 1950s and 1960s, we are used to cooking meals from scratch rather than having microwavable ready-meals. However, what can happen with retirement is that we may eat too well. More meals out and nice home-cooked meals with a bottle of wine most nights. We can, of course, continue to eat out, eat and drink what we enjoy, with a focus on health being secondary. We all have choices. But it may be worth reflecting on what we eat; should we go for at least two days a week without alcohol and maybe keep the wine to a glass of red with a healthy meal?

2. Be active

It's less about exercise and more about physical activity.

Being active can have a positive impact on brain health and cognition and reduce the risk of dementia. It can also help to reduce stress, improve anxiety and depression, and can help us to sleep better. The World Health Organisation has identified physical inactivity as the fourth leading risk factor for global mortality. Inactive lifestyles are also a proven risk factor in a range of chronic health conditions including heart attacks, strokes, type-2 diabetes, and depression. Being more active can prevent all of these and will also reduce the risk of frailty in old age.

There's an interesting study from the 1950s comparing the deaths of 5,000 men with desk-based and those with more-active jobs. Bus drivers were more likely to die earlier than bus conductors, who were going up and down stairs each day. And more desk-based post-office workers died of heart attacks than postal delivery workers.

Physical activity has many benefits for cardiovascular health. It promotes blood flow, reduces the risk of clots in the arteries, and strengthens the heart muscle. This results in a lower heart rate, less pressure on the heart, and decreased blood pressure. Additionally, regular physical activity can raise levels of good cholesterol, which can help prevent the thickening of the arteries. It also benefits mental and brain health. Most jobs involve a lot of sitting, and then we go to the gym for a burst of exercise. But we don't need to go to the gym; we can add more activity into our day, through carrying shopping and other household chores.

Whilst walking is good, we also need to do some resistance exercise to strengthen our muscles, as, from the age of 40, each year we lose almost 2 per cent of muscle mass and strength. I do weight training at the gym twice a week and spend at least one day a week moving logs and branches at the wood, the equivalent of a day in the garden as I move my wheelbarrow.

There are many role models of people who are outstanding for their age, such as Aleksander Doba who, at 67, completed the longest open-water kayaking expedition across the Atlantic; Ernestine Shepherd, who, at 87, is the worlds' oldest living female competitive bodybuilder; and Orville Rogers, who was still breaking track records at 100. But it's just as useful to go to dance classes or the gym and we can see much older people working out and having fun.

Find your balance

As we age, balance can become a significant issue, leading to falls which are the leading cause of accidental deaths and fractures among older adults. Unfortunately, many individuals who experience a hip fracture never fully recover their independence or vitality. One easy and effective way to improve balance is to practice standing on one leg while performing everyday tasks such as brushing your teeth or waiting for the kettle to boil. The goal is to be able to stand on one leg for 30 seconds with eyes open and 10 seconds with eyes closed, with the assistance of something to hold onto if needed.

What works for me is to walk while I'm on the phone, dance while the kettle is boiling or I'm waiting for a pan to boil, and to stand on one leg while I clean my teeth. I also make sure I move for 5 minutes every hour; my watch buzzes to remind me and with my office on the second floor of my home, I do a lot of stair walking.

3. Sleep well

Sleep is important; it improves cognitive functioning and memory, and it balances our insulin function and glucose intake. Sleep can also reduce the risk of anxiety, depression, PTSD, and the long-term effects of grief. It does this by helping us to process difficult emotions and experiences, giving us a better chance of staying resilient, positive, and happy.

Lack of sleep is linked to an increased risk of high blood pressure and ischemic heart disease, due to the accumulation of amyloid deposits that clog the arteries. Proper sleep is also crucial for effective blood flow in the brain, which in turn reduces the risk of stroke and vascular dementia.

Standard wisdom is that we all need seven to nine hours sleep a night to maintain our immune system and fight infection, but people differ; for some six may be enough, and others may need ten. In retirement people are likely to sleep for 20 minutes longer and have improved quality of sleep.[26] Retirees reported fewer early morning awakenings and feeling more refreshed after a night's sleep.

I've checked with an expert, and they tell me that for a good nights' sleep we should keep physically active; go to bed and get up at the same time each day; keep the bedroom cool and dark; avoid caffeine after 2 pm and limit alcohol consumption. She also said spending some time each day outside in natural light will ensure our body gets a good dose of the melatonin that it needs for us to sleep well. This also triggers our natural body clock, helping us sleep better.

4. Manage stress/mental well-being

Before retirement, many people are so focused on work they don't actually realise they are stressed; it has become the norm. Discrimination, bullying, poverty, and poor housing can all contribute to feeling stressed. Others recognise its importance and start paying more attention to their bodies and realise the importance of managing mental health. The transition to retirement can be stressful, with the uncertainty of letting go and what comes next. I covered this in Chapter 2.

With an increasing number of people suffering from stress, depression, and anxiety, the other aspects of health can all help. Taking a holistic view means that we pay attention to what we eat, how active we are, the amount of sleep we get, having healthy relationships and avoiding substance abuse. Having a clear purpose and having a meaningful life will improve our mental health. Having someone to talk with can give us a different perspective, lower cortisol, and reduce stress.

At points in the day we can pause, take three deep breaths and savour the moment. We don't need to be busy all the time, and with retirement, people can assume we have time for their priorities; make sure you focus on what you want to do. You don't have to say yes to everything.

I'm an advocate for spending more time out in nature. Being outdoors and listening to the sound of birds, the wind in the trees, and feeling the ground under foot can help to clear our mind, as can gardening. Spending time in the natural world reduces stress and results in a feeling of being in control and takes us away from our problems. A research paper analysed 22 studies on gardening and health, comparing those who garden with those who don't. There was a wide range of health benefits, including reductions in depression, anxiety, and BMI, plus a rise in life satisfaction and quality of life. As I finish this chapter, I'll be off to the wood, with my phone on silent.

5. Relationships

I talk more about relationships in Chapter 7, but for now I want to emphasise the importance of relationships for our health and longevity. We laugh more when we're with friends and this is good for our circulation and digestion. This lowers the stress hormones cortisol and adrenaline (by up to 70 per cent) and stabilises blood sugars and insulin, regulates blood pressure, and reduces inflammation. Friendships increase our cognitive reserve and create new neurons which help avoid dementia, Alzheimer's, and reduce stress. People who enjoyed strong social bonds into their 80s were less likely to succumb to cognitive decline and dementia and were also protected against vascular diseases. A six-year study of 736 middle-aged Swedish men[27] found having a life partner didn't affect the risk of heart attack or fatal coronary heart disease, but having friends did.

Other people can be a cause of stress. As we age, we can be more selective with whom we spend our time; we can avoid those who seek to bring us down. I enjoy time alone, and there is a difference between spending time alone and being lonely. Loneliness has been linked to numerous negative health outcomes, including increased mortality rates. Studies[28] have shown that the impact of loneliness on health is similar to the negative effects of smoking and excessive alcohol consumption, and even surpasses the risks associated with obesity. Chronic loneliness can contribute to the development of mental health conditions, cardiovascular disease (increasing the risk of heart attack and strokes by 30 per cent), and a weakened immune system, among other health problems. It's important for individuals to take steps to reduce feelings of loneliness and maintain social connections for their physical and mental well-being.

Intimacy

Intimacy encompasses more than just sexual activity; it also involves physical touch and affectionate gestures such as hugs and caresses. A study of nearly 7,000 individuals aged between 50 and 90 found that older adults who were sexually active had better cognitive abilities in areas of memory and planning.[29] Engaging in intimate relationships releases endorphins, which can increase feelings of happiness. The research also showed that being single and not engaging in sexual activity does not necessarily result in dissatisfaction as long as an individual is content with their single status. However, dissatisfaction with sexual experiences within a relationship can led to unhappiness.

6. Avoid risky substances

We can be addicted to alcohol, tobacco, prescription drugs, porn, gambling, and excessive online and social media use. All can have a negative impact on our health and relationships. We know that smoking is the biggest risk factor in developing cancer and can put us at greater risk of heart disease. It can also reduce our life expectancy by 15 years or more. Drinking too much can lead to chronic liver disease, some cancers, and heart disease. Social media can give us a dopamine hit and we can become addicted to 'likes'. It's worth monitoring your use across these areas and to see which are part of a healthy life and which are a way of dealing with stress. There are healthier ways to manage stress, described earlier in this chapter: physical activity, healthy eating, meditation, social relationships, and connecting with nature.

7. Meaning and purpose

Having a sense of purpose and engaging in creative activities can benefit our overall health. The act of creating art, whether it be through painting, poetry, sculpting or baking, not only improves our mood, but also strengthens and forms new connections between brain cells, thus improving cognitive function.[30] It can also help us to better deal with stress. This is such an important aspect to our adjustment to retirement that you will find it covered in depth in Section 3.

ON DEATH

I watched a moving interview[31] with Daniel Friedland, MD, who was diagnosed with cancer and sadly died. He spoke about how first thoughts are often around 'Why me?' and 'Why now?' He said that a better question could be 'What matters right now?' – and to be more in the moment. Daniel wrote that when he asked himself the question about what mattered most, right now, he had a shift of energy in his body and he set to focus more on making every moment count; to appreciate others and to focus on relationships.

BEFORE YOU MOVE ON …

This has been a detailed chapter, with plenty to get you thinking. As we end this chapter, I'd like you to consider these two questions:

1. Imagine that you are your healthiest self, or a role model. What would you or they say to you about your health, your activity, your ability to deal with stress etc.?
2. What can you do today to look after yourself better?

You may like to write your answers in your journal and perhaps talk about this with your reflections buddy.

NOTES

1 Dewe, P., & Kompier, M. (2008) *Foresight Mental Capital and Well-being Project. Well-being and Work: Future Challenges.* The Government Office for Science, London

2 Rosenthal, D., & Moore, S. (2018). *The Psychology of Retirement.* Routledge, New York.

3 Hessel, P., & Bell Fellow, D.E. (2016). Does retirement (really) lead to worse health among European men and women across all educational levels? *Social Science & Medicine.*

4 Eibich, P. (2015). Understanding the effect of retirement on health: Mechanisms and heterogeneity. *Journal of Health Economics*, 43, 1–12.

5 van der Heide, I., van Rijn, R.M., & Robroek, S.J. (2013). Is retirement good for your health? A systematic review of longitudinal studies. *BMC Public Health* 13, 1180.

6 Kim, J.E., & Moen, P. (2001). Moving into retirement: Preparation and transitions in late midlife. In M.E. Lachman (Ed.), *Handbook of Midlife Development* (487–527). John Wiley, New York.

7 Mein, G., Martikainen, P., Hemingway, H., Stansfeld, S., & Marmot, M. (2003). Is retirement good or bad for mental and physical health functioning? Whitehall longitudinal study of civil servants. *Journal of Epidemiology and Community Health*, 57(1), 46–49.

8 Wang, M. (2007). Profiling retirees in the retirement transition and adjustment process: Examining the longitudinal change patterns of retirees' psychological well-being. *Journal of Applied Psychology*, 92, 455–474.

9 Holmes, T.H., & Rahe, R.H. (1967). The social readjustment rating scale. *Journal of Psychosomatic Research*, 11, 213–218.

10 Van Solinge, H., & Henkens, K. (2008). Adjustment to and satisfaction with retirement: Two of a kind? *Psychology and Aging*, 23(2), 422–434.

11 Moon, J.R., Glymour, M.M., Subramanian, S., Avendaño, M., & Kawachi, I. (2012). Transition to retirement and risk of cardiovascular disease: Prospective analysis of the US health and retirement study. *Social Science & Medicine*, 75(3), 526–530.

12 Dave, D., Rashad, I., & Spasojevic, J. (2008). The effects of retirement on physical and mental outcomes. *Southern Economic Journal*, 75, 497–523.

13 Kim, J. E. & Moen, P. (2002). Retirement transitions, gender, and psychological well-being: A life-course, ecological model. *Journals of Gerontology: Psychological Sciences*, 57B, 212–222.

14 Calvo, E., Haverstick, K., & Sass, S.A. (2009). Gradual retirement, sense of control, and retirees' happiness. *Research on Aging*, 31, 112–135.

15 Bleidorn, W., & Schwaba, T. (2018). Retirement is associated with change in self-esteem. *Psychology and Aging*, 33, 586–594.

16 Burr, A., Santo, J., & Pushkar, D. (2011). Affective well-being in retirement: The influence of values, money, and health across three years. *Journal of Happiness Studies*, 12(1), 17–40.

17 Bosse, R., Aldwin, C.M., Levenson, M.R., & Workman-Daniels, K. (1991). How stressful is retirement? Findings from the normative aging study. *Journal of Gerontology*, 46(1), 9–14.

18 van Solinge, H. (2012). Adjustment to retirement. In M. Wang (Ed.), *Oxford Handbook of Retirement* (311–324). Oxford University Press, Oxford.

19 DWP, YouGov PLC, (2015). DWP ad hoc research report no. 15. *Attitudes of the over 50s to Fuller Working Lives*. ISBN 978-1-78425-432-2.

20 https://tilda.tcd.ie

21 Levy, B., (2022) *Breaking the Age Code*. Ebury.

22 Perls, E. https://www.bumc.bu.edu/centenarian/

23 Seligman, M. (2011). *Flourish*. Nicholas Brealey Publishing.

24 Gratton, L., & Scott, A. (2016). *The 100-Year Life: Living and Working in an Age of Longevity*. Bloomsbury Publishing.

25 Eggar, G., Binns, A., Rosser, S., & Sagner, M. (2017). *Lifestyle Medicine* (3rd ed.). Academic Press, London.

26 Myllyntausta, S., Salo, P., Kronholm, E., Pentti, J., Kivimäki, M., Vahtera, J., Stenholm, S. (2017). Changes in sleep difficulties during the transition to statutory retirement. *Sleep*.

27 Orth-Gomér, K., Rosengren, A., Wilhelmsen, L., Orth-Gomér, K., Rosengren, A., & Wilhelmsen, L. (1993). Lack of social support and incidence of coronary heart disease in middle-aged Swedish men. *Psychosomatic Medicine*, 55(1), 37–43.

28 Holt-Lunstad, J., Smith, T. B., Baker, M., Harris, T., & Stephenson, D. (2015). Loneliness and social isolation as risk factors for mortality: A meta-analytic review. *Perspectives on Psychological Science*, 10(2), 227–237.

29 Kenny, R.A. (2022). *Age Proof: The New Science of Living a Longer and Healthier Life*. Lagom.

30 Ibid.

31 *Growing Wiser through Challenging Transition*. https://youtu.be/RAPnQkp87Fs

7

RELATIONSHIPS

Why you should read this chapter

We have relationships with our partner/spouse, with our parents, our children, other family members, work colleagues, friends and acquaintances, and the wider community. However, of all the relationships we have, the most important one is the one that we have with ourselves. We are the only person who is with us from birth to death, and unless we are happy with ourselves, we will never be happy with anyone else. Referring back to Chapter 4, where we looked inwards, and Chapter 5, about work, will remind you of your strengths. Being happy with who we are will help if we seek to build friendships and perhaps new romantic relationships; we are more likely to come across as approachable and thus achieve our aims. The chapter will start with the importance of relationships and group membership for retirement.

A happy and fulfilling life is not based on career success, money in the bank, healthy eating, but with our relationships with others. The more meaningful our connections with others, the more likely we are to live happy, satisfying, and overall healthier lives.[1] Just like the need for continued physical fitness, we also need social fitness and to take care of our relationships through regular contact. Let's now look at different relationships.

DOI: 10.4324/9781003374206-9

GROUP MEMBERSHIP

Membership of a group – such as the family, or sports or leisure groups – can help us adjust to retirement; being part of a group helps us with our social identity and to know who we are.[2] We need to belong to more than one group, however, to provide us with more psychological resources, such as a sense of belonging, emotional support, enhanced self-esteem, trust, and positive affect and this helps us to deal with life's challenges; it can be draining and stressful when you always turn to the same person.[3] We may find that a family group is an important source of emotional support, and an interest group (such as my comedy improv group) may help to provide us with a sense of commonality with others.

A study of 171 recently retired Australians found that having multiple group memberships is a crucial factor in determining health perception, quality of life, and overall adjustment. Being a part of multiple groups improves retirement outcomes as it gives retirees a chance to continue making a positive impact in others' lives by offering support and feeling valuable.

As we approach retirement, we should review the groups we belong to and seek to maintain any positive group membership, for example, through a sports group, and also join groups outside of the workplace. When joining a new group, we may like to consider the makeup; it is beneficial to meet people across the ages, not just those of a similar age.

Activity 7.1

Make a note in your journal of the groups you belong to. Given the benefits of belonging to multiple groups, should you seek to join more? How many people would you class as people you can talk to about your personal life? If the answer is no one or just one person, how could you expand on this? You can then discuss this with your reflections buddy.

RELATIONSHIPS ARE THE BIGGEST
PREDICTOR OF LIFELONG HEALTH

Being in a loving relationship helps our health; whilst this could be with our romantic partner, it could also be with close friends, and an unhappy relationship can have a negative impact on our health. Strong relationships help to guard against depression and reduces stress; those with close friends are nearly a third less likely to suffer heart disease or strokes, and friendships can even help reduce physical pain too. It's less about the number of people and more about the strength of relationships. We need people that we could call on in need, even if it is in the middle of the night. These are the people who help us to deal better with the stressors of life.[4]

Many studies have shown that being socially connected to others is positively related to happiness, and indeed being alone in the world or being lonely is generally a strong detriment to happiness.[5] Social connections are also important to meaningfulness, and most people's reports on what makes their lives meaningful feature relationships with family and friends.[6] But we need more than one relationship and different people can meet different needs. This is why, as well as these deep connections, there is also a need for a breadth of relationships, reminding us of when we were teenagers, rather than relying on just a couple of people.

Activity 7.2

The relationship map – Write down the names of your family, friends, and acquaintances on small pieces of paper. Put yourself in the centre and then pick up each piece of paper in turn to position them. Put those closest to you, in real life, close to you and those who are more like acquaintances, further away. It helps to do this twice, (take a photo after the first time); once with how things are right now, and then to do it again, imagining life a couple of years after retirement as you expect life to be. Are you likely to have made new friends and gained a wider number of acquaintances or will things have contracted? Looking at the future, to what extent are you happy with this?

Then think about the people you know; do you have people with whom you can do different activities; for example, to go to events with – theatre, concerts, gigs, hikes, and also shopping, talk to, hug, contact when in need, have fun, have a laugh with and someone who you can help, and who helps you feel needed. It may be useful to write down the names against each activity. If you spot a gap, you can look for opportunities for someone to perhaps go to the theatre with if it is not your partner's thing.

OUR RELATIONSHIP WITH OURSELVES

Do you like yourself? Are you happy with the person you are? I've worked with clients who are not happy with themselves and focus on the negative, all the things they aren't. We can compare 'our inside to others outside' – this is where we consider our actual life with the highly curated life that people share on social media. But this is highly curated. Other people are probably not having as much fun as they would have you believe. Taking a negative view can mean we talk to ourselves in a critical way – telling ourselves that we are useless and that no one likes us. As you notice yourself talking to yourself in this way, try to be more kind – you are not an idiot for making a mistake, no one is perfect. We should aim to like ourselves for the people we are, to embrace our quirks, and perhaps seek out situations where our style of being is welcomed. Return to Chapters 4 and 5 to remind yourself of your strengths.

Activity 7.3

I'd like you to journal on how much you like yourself, and you do not need to share this with anyone. It can help to be fully open, as later you can review it and it may give you suggestions on small changes you can make to your thoughts and behaviours.

Time alone and loneliness

Loneliness is defined as a subjective sense of distress and discomfort with one's social ties.[7] If we are lonely, we can be more likely to experience depression on retirement, so joining groups and focus on connections is beneficial for our health. Research[8] found that some older adults reported feeling most peaceful in solitude; this is different to being lonely. Some of us are introverts, and don't need a large number of friends; we are happy with time alone. It is time with our thoughts, to enable us to recharge. When we choose time alone, we can maintain high levels of well-being.

ROMANTIC RELATIONSHIPS

Over the almost 40 years I've been running pre-retirement seminars, one question that is often raised is over the impact of retirement on a couples' relationship. Forty years ago, the majority had traditional relationships, generally with a wife as homemaker and the husband going out to work. With both likely to be at home, as well as deciding on who does which of the family chores there was also a concern over more time spent together. There's an old saying – 'For better or for worse but not for lunch.' 'He's going to be under my feet' was a common fear back in the 1980s.

There is mixed evidence on the question of whether people who are married or live together adjust better to retirement than those who are not. Some research shows that having a marital partner can contribute positively to life satisfaction and adjustment in general,[9,10] but not always. Partly this is down to the quality of the relationship, and many long-term relationships can be stressful as people have grown apart.

At this stage of life, we have adjustment to retirement and also the adjustment to spending more time together. This adjustment can take time, so be ready for some challenges along the way. If one half of the couple has been focused on work with few outside interests, they can assume that all their needs will be met from their partner. It is helpful to build up a social network before retirement, as otherwise the partner (usually the woman) can find herself having to plan activities for their partner too, which can lead to difficulties in their relationship.

There is no one perfect way to be a couple after full-time work. Some will want to follow traditional roles. Others may want to make changes, and a conversation can cover how much time to spend together. Couples are likely to have differing priorities and attitudes about retirement. It is healthy to spend time apart, reducing resentment and bringing something back into the relationship. And, whilst for many a marriage gets better after retirement, this isn't true for all; for others it is an ending and a transition to becoming a 'silver splitter'.

No longer do people live together as the standard. There are people who are in a committed relationship but live in separate homes, often at a distance. Vanda lives in London and her partner in the north of England, and they visit each other regularly. Neither wanted to move away from friends and family, and this works for them. George and Sally live in the same apartment block; it's where they met, but they love having their own places even though they spend much of their time together.

My aim in writing this chapter is for you to have the conversation with your partner about what you expect from the relationship moving forward. Too many of us make assumptions. Jim wanted breakfast to continue at 07.30 each morning just like when he went to work. Mary wanted more time to paint and for Jim to make his own breakfast! We may have differing views on what a typical day would be like, when you would eat together, who does what household chores, and the amount of alone time you need. If one half of the couple has an active social life, will their partner be able to join in or would it be better for them to cultivate their own interests?

Considering the wider family, are others making assumptions about time spent with grandchildren? Jim agreed to look after the grandchildren two days a week before discussing it with Mary. He didn't actually mean for him to look after them and assumed Mary would take on this role, but whilst Mary loved her grandchildren, she wanted retirement to give her time to paint. Without clear communication, it caused friction within the family that could have been avoided if this conversation had happened earlier.

Activity 7.4

Answer these questions individually and then discuss your answers together:

- What does your ideal daily and weekly routine in retirement look like?
- How many friends do you plan to spend time with?

- What role will you play with your grandchildren?
- What healthy habits do you hope to incorporate into your retirement?
- How do you plan to handle unexpected expenses and events in retirement?
- What plans have you put in place for financial protection in case of death or incapacity?

BEING SINGLE

Not everyone is part of a couple. Some are single from choice; others would love to have a romantic relationship. When single, I had a good social life and worked on building friendships. Once I started dating, I still maintained those friendships. Living, now, with my partner, it remains important that I spend time with friends. It is worth reflecting on how happy you are at the moment and if you should consider dating.

I could write a book on my experiences of dating post 60, and it can be a challenge to put yourself out there after a long relationship. It was important to me to find myself first, and to be happy to go to places alone. I then went on many dates, as I had no idea as to what type of person was right for me. I listened to too many people who advised me to wear makeup, and to present myself in a way that would appeal to more men, but I'm not a woman who wears makeup and heels. And then it clicked. Just be me. So, no hiding my size, going makeup free, and giving a clear idea of the person I was. It was the photo of me chopping wood that made my partner stop and think this person is a bit different and he swiped right!

I didn't want a pen pal, and many I matched with never wanted to meet (I later found out they were probably married and seeking validation). I found a walk in the park was less stressful than a meal out. Afterwards, I'd take some time to reflect on how I felt with them and whether I'd want to meet a second time. I recognised that when people are nervous, they talk about themselves but for me it was important to feel listened to and more energised with them than de-energised.

I wanted to find out if our values were aligned, which was more important than the same taste in music.

According to research, older adults rate honesty, communication, companionship, respect, and positive attitude as the top five elements of successful romantic relationships, while younger adults rate love, communication, trust, attraction, and compatibility as the most important factors for relationship success. Honesty is around truthful confiding, which involves vulnerability but fosters intimacy when done mindfully and sensitively. It's worth looking again at your top values from Chapter 4 so you can use them if you re-enter the dating world.

FAMILY RELATIONSHIPS – PARENTS AND CHILDREN

We are likely to have a much wider family than parents, children, and siblings; we can be part of blended families. The death of a parent can mean that we are now the matriarch or patriarch of the family and seen by others as responsible for maintaining family transitions. There are more estrangements, too, affecting one in five families. We can find ourselves caught in the middle of caring for elderly parents and still supporting our children. We also can be grandparents and involved in the care of grandchildren.

Talking with clients and participants on my workshops, there are fewer people who have the traditional family set up and many wish it was different than it is. We can work on our relationships and seek therapy and counselling to address aspects of our past, but we can't make anyone want to do something. With ageing parents, we may need to devote more time to their care, and our children may still have a call on us. We can choose what we say yes to; like Jim and Mary above, don't say yes on behalf of someone else, and make sure you do what is right for you; if not there can be resentments.

FRIENDS AND ACQUAINTANCES

Work colleagues

For many, work provides a sense of belonging and community and when leaving our work, we lose this connection. As we plan for retirement it is useful to decide how we will fill this need, and this can be by joining communities of interest through religion, hobbies, learning, or volunteering. The year or more leading up to retirement can focus on building other relationships and interests, so there is not the feeling of loss and being too reliant on your partner.

Friendships

As children, we make friends at school, in the playground, through our sports and other interests. Later we make friends through work and by meeting the parents of our children's friends, but it can get more difficult later in life. Indeed, when surveying people before retirement they think a reliable income is what they will miss most when retired, but after retirement they say it is the social connections; this is where volunteering can fill the gap. As in a new romantic relationship, we want friends who bring out the best in us, who support and encourage us.

We need to work on our friendships. Leaving my marriage, I didn't have a single friend, and set out to make some. It was hard work, but I put in effort, made sure to make time for them and continue to reach out and be in touch on a regular basis. It doesn't always have to be face to face; we can talk via WhatsApp and at least send messages. I've built strong relationships with people I only meet on Zoom via a group I belong too, and prior to lockdown would not have thought that this could be satisfying, but it is. Many of us meet friends for specific things, such as to go to a dance, to the theatre, but just hanging out is beneficial, meeting for a coffee and a chat, or a walk in the park.

You may like to consider a review of your friendships. Earlier I asked if you had people to do different things with. Now I'd like you to consider which of them energise you and which drain your energy. Sometimes we need to let go of some friends who take up too much of our energy to allow space for meeting new people. Our interests can change; I used to spend a lot of time with my dance friends, but a knee injury meant I had to give up dancing and my friends changed to people I met at gigs.

Activity 7.5

Make a list of the people that you know and, besides each, note whether they drain your energy (energy vampire) or energise you.

Name	Energy vampire	Neutral	Energiser

Casual encounters and the wider community

We meet people in our day-to-day lives, at the shop, as the postal worker delivers our mail, walking; these are people we exchange brief pleasantries with. We recognise their existence, and them us, and this gives us a sense of well-being. Our wider circle of contacts can include the staff at our regular coffee shop and familiar faces at the gym. We can meet people in many ways – sitting on a park bench, meeting dog walkers, in a coffee shop. These are all places where we can start a conversation. There are also meetup groups, church groups, yoga classes etc. Many of the people we meet have the potential to become our friends.

IMPROVING RELATIONSHIPS

Moving in with someone in my 60s has given me a personal interest in improving relationships. Researching, I found that we should spend at least five times as much time celebrating as arguing, and we should take an active constructive approach to how we reply.

For example, our partner has some good news which they share; we can ignore them completely and ask about some household tasks (passive destructive). We can give a bland 'Well done' (which is passively constructive) but what works much better is to ask them to tell you about the emotions they felt when they found this out, which is actively constructive.

Some people like to talk, and whilst they may have interesting things to say, other people can see them as uninterested in them. We need to aim to balance the amount of time we talk and listen. When we meet someone, we should think about being a good listener and to be fully present. We can help by asking open questions rather than thinking and planning what we will say next. We can then reply based on what is said. We should also remember that unless people ask for it, they don't want someone to tell them what to do. We should keep our advice to ourselves and encourage and support them to find the right answer for themselves.

The nature of emotions

Sometimes it can be hard to name how we feel, and we can be 'wound up' by others. What can help is to pause and to notice what emotions are arising. Process that before responding and you are less likely to have a regret or to escalate the situation. When people have a different view to us, rather than seek challenge and conflict, we can be curious. We can share our thoughts more tentatively when someone asks us an opinion on a political matter. We can also be more focused on understanding than trying to win.

Activity 7.6

We may have our own view of these questions, but what can be helpful is to ask these questions of someone we trust. We need to be aware that we may not like the reply, but it helps us to develop and grow. Barry found it hard to hear that he turned every conversation around to himself; he thought this was adding to a conversation, but others told him they felt he wasn't interested in them. He heard this from three different people so realised he needed to change. Your reflections buddy may be the first person to ask these questions; who else will you ask?

- Am I easy to get along with?
- Am I aware of the people around me?
- Do I listen enough?
- Am I open-minded?

- Am I judgemental or defensive?
- Am I difficult to approach or reactive around certain topics?

You may like to reflect on the answers in your journal and make some plans.

ENDINGS, DEATH, AND DYING

As I end this chapter on relationships it is important to include the end of relationships. With friendships, and romantic relationships, sometimes we outgrow each other and we, or they, decide it is time to move on. There is also the death of our partner/spouse, which can lead to a void and loneliness; it can be hard to do things alone when you have always done things as a couple. Additionally, there is loss of intimacy, someone to touch and kiss. With age come more and more losses, of other family members and friends. The media each day tells us of another actor or musician who has died, and these are often people we grew up watching or listening to.

As we age, we inevitably experience loss of loved ones and friends. We need to be allowed to mourn those losses, but also be allowed to retain emotional bonds with people who have passed away. Our sense of identity is collective, and when we lose a loved one we also lose a piece of who we were in relation to them. It can be really important to have re-membering practices where we remember and connect with those we have lost and remember how we used to feel in their presence.

Activity 7.7

I'd like you to consider a way of honouring and remembering people who are close in your life. It could be to spend reflection time at the grave-side. It may be a celebration of their life with other family members. You may like to have a quiet time to recall things you did together and the person they were. Some people will send a personalised Christmas card out, perhaps showing you both as a couple. Put a note inside to say why you are doing this. Why not talk with your reflections buddy about someone important to you that is no longer here.

BEFORE YOU MOVE ON …

As we end this chapter, I'd like you to consider how happy you are with your relationships; think about the people in your lives. Choose a couple of people and for each, think of one thing you can do to enhance the relationship. It could be to listen more, to pick up the phone for a chat or plan a time to meet. I'd also like you, if you want to expand your friendship group, to identify a good place to meet people, either formally or where you may be more likely to bump into people who share your interests. You may like to write your answers in your journal and perhaps talk about this with your reflections buddy.

NOTES

1 Waldinger, R., & Schulz, M. (2023). *The Good Life.* Simon & Schuster.
2 Tajfel, H., & Turner, J.C. (1979). An integrative theory of intergroup conflict. In W.G. Austin & S. Worchel (Eds.), *The Social Psychology of Intergroup Relations* (33–47). Brooks-Cole, Monterey, CA.
3 Jetten, J., Haslam, C., Haslam, S.A., Dingle, G., & Jones, J. M. (2014). How groups affect our health and well-being: the path from theory to policy. *Social Issues and Policy Review*, 8, 103–130.
4 Dr. Robert J. Waldinger, director of the Harvard Study of Adult Development.
5 Cacioppo, J.T., & Patrick, W. (2008). *Loneliness: Human Nature and the Need for Social Connection.* W. W. Norton & Co.
6 Debats, D.L. (1999). Sources of meaning: An investigation of significant commitments in life. *Journal of Humanistic Psychology*, 39(4), 30–57.
7 Andersson, L. (1998). Loneliness research and interventions: A review of the literature. *Aging & Mental Health*, 2(4), 264–274.
8 Weinstein, N., Nguyen, T., & Hansen, H., (2021) What time alone offers: Narratives of solitude from adolescence to older adulthood. *Frontiers in Psychology*, 12.
9 Etaugh, C., & Bridges, J. (2013). *Women's Lives: A Psychological Perspective* (3rd ed.). Allyn and Bacon, Boston, MA.
10 Trudel, G., Boyer, R., Villeneuve, V., Anderson, A., Pilon, G., & Bounader, J. (2008). The marital life and aging well program: Effects of a group preventive intervention on the marital and sexual functioning of retired couples. *Sexual Relationship Therapy*, 23, 5–23.

8

FINANCIAL WELL-BEING

Why you should read this chapter

Financial well-being is integral to general well-being. I've taken a psychological perspective and made practical suggestions. We need to consider our future: how much will be enough and alternative ways of getting that money, so this chapter links to Chapter 5 about work. Many younger people see all pensioners as wealthy, but there are many with limited financial resources, so we need to ensure we have all the benefits we are entitled to. We need to be clear on how much we spend, and if we can make any changes now. I also raise the need for a will and the relevance of lasting powers of attorney (LPAs).

Financial well-being is linked to general well-being and is an important resource as we move into this next stage of life. It covers the ability to pay our monthly bills, how we manage savings and debt, and how our relationship with money fits in with a meaningful life. I wondered about the need for this chapter, as there is so much available elsewhere regarding pensions, savings etc., so this is very much the view of a psychologist who is now close to receiving her state pension. I'm based in the UK, and I appreciate you may live in another country; I encourage you to find advice that relates to where you live.

SAVING FOR RETIREMENT

I read many academic articles on this topic – one from the United States focused on the role of psychology as to whether

DOI: 10.4324/9781003374206-10

or not people save for retirement. Research found that some people could have saved more for retirement but chose to spend instead, focusing on the present rather than on the future. If you can't imagine the future, there is no urgency to save for it. We put it off, and then we are still in the present when we review again. This is relevant to a wider view on retirement; we can imagine, or not, what our life will be like ten or more years into the future.

Studies by economists have revealed that only a small fraction of working individuals who reach retirement age have accumulated assets worth more than twice their pre-retirement annual income,[1] and even that is not enough for a comfortable retirement. Many procrastinate rather than start saving for retirement as they join the workforce. If you were a procrastinator, you may find you need to work for longer, to meet your savings goals. As mentioned above, people are more likely to save for the future if they have a future time perspective and enjoy thinking and planning for the future.

There are nearly two million people aged 55 to 64 who do not have any private pension savings; fewer than 48 per cent of these own their homes outright and nearly a quarter are still renting; 10 per cent of those aged 65 and over still have a mortgage. This is a large number of people who will need to carry on earning, and so remaining in good health and finding work is important.

Activity 8.1

I'd like you to take time to imagine your future retirement. What do you see yourself doing, and how much money are you likely to need? How does this relate to your pension provision and other savings? I'll be taking you into more depth on this throughout this chapter, but it will be helpful to capture your initial thoughts into your journal and to arrange a discussion with your reflections buddy.

There are many younger people who seek financial independence to retire early (FIRE) and this is in order to have autonomy to do what they want. We all need enough money to pay our bills but most of us want more than a basic lifestyle. We want to be able to drive a car (unless we live in a large city), have a holiday, meals out. But how much do we actually need?

I work with clients whose yearly salary is well into six figures but who feel that this is not enough, and others whose income is low, but they are content. Some are driven by events from childhood and the need for security; others continually compare themselves to their contemporaries.

Activity 8.2

Let's take a view on your financial well-being. We should have the equivalent of six months' salary as a 'rainy-day' fund to cover the cost of a boiler replacement and other unexpected bills. In retirement, alongside our state retirement pension, we may have an occupational or personal pension and savings. Will you have enough to finance the life you want? Look back at your answers to the questions on financial well-being in Chapter 3 and then rate yourself using this scale.

How would you rate your financial well-being on a 1–10 scale? (10 is high)

1 – 2 – 3 – 4 – 5 – 6 – 7 – 8 – 9 – 10

Now, whatever your score, what could you do to raise it by 1? List three action steps you could take to improve your score – this could be to generate more income or to reduce expenditure. Which of these are you willing to start with today? Write it down.

HOW MUCH DO YOU NEED?

Financial planning for retirement often focuses on levels of savings, but how much we expect to spend is as important. Three in ten people from the UK aged 55 to 64 do not have any pension savings at all and less than 40 per cent of people understand how much money they will need in retirement. Talking to the UK government-funded free service Money Helper (previously called Pension Wise) can help understand your position.

Whilst many find it boring, taking time to understand current expenditure and how much you will need in retirement is sensible. We know about our regular payments such as rent/mortgage, council tax, utilities, food, broadband/phone, TV licence, and transport. We then need clothes, money to go out and for holidays, money to pay for the dentist and medicines. But we also have unexpected expenses, such as if we urgently need to replace the boiler or significant repairs on the car. Too many, when asked, say they will deal with it when it happens. You can access a budget planner from the Money Saving Expert website.

How will your spending change in retirement?

When we retire, there will be less need for work clothes, and we will save on commuting costs, plus the regular contributions to buy presents for colleagues. On the other hand, we are likely to go out more and maybe plan to eat out more, too. If we spend more time at home it will impact on heating costs. This is why it is sensible to track our level of expenditure. If we pay for membership of an expensive sports club, what would it be like to use a cheaper one? Prior to retirement we can look into perhaps keeping our car longer, rather than changing it every three years. We can also see what it is like to opt for more affordable seats at the theatre.

If we have debt

Many people think that in our 60s we will be comfortably off, but Lucy and Wilf had a combination of business failure, health problems, and a loan to a family member that was not repaid. They used Step Change (a non-profit organisation offering debt counselling and practical support for managing debts) to manage their debt and to help them to deal with their creditors.

RETIREMENT LIVING STANDARDS

These are reviewed regularly to ensure they are in line with changes in expectations of what people need and the rising cost of goods and services. As I go to press, the cost of a minimum lifestyle for a single person increased from £10,900 to £12,800 (18%); and for a couple from £16,700 to £19,900 (19%). This includes £96 for a couple's weekly food shop, a week's holiday in the UK, eating out about once a month, and some affordable leisure activities about twice a week. It does not include running a car.

A moderate retirement income is now £23,300 for a single retiree and £34,000 for a couple. This includes spending £127 on a weekly shop, a two-week holiday in Europe, and eating out a few times a month. As a couple, for a comfortable lifestyle in retirement, you need an annual joint income of more than £54,000, which will give you £238 a week for a food shop, regular beauty treatments, trips to the theatre, and three weeks' holiday in Europe. For a single person it is £37,300. These examples assume we are mortgage free.

If you are renting or continue to pay a mortgage you will need more than this, although there are also state benefits available. It's a wakeup call to many, but we can continue working longer before we start taking a personal pension and continue with some work into later life.

PENSIONS

Occupational and personal pension

Fewer people than previously have a defined-benefit pension. For those that do, and have worked for many years with the same organisation, they are likely to have a comfortable retirement, often with a pension of up to half their salary alongside a lump sum.

More people are on defined-contribution pensions, with less certainty. With auto-enrolment, the Government has been encouraging people to start a pension, such as via NEST, or you may have created your own, but for many this will only provide a small addition to the state pension. There are options to how you take your pension pot, which I'll leave for you to discuss with financial organisations and to review the information on the Money Helper website. You may have some 'lost pensions' from previous jobs. The Money Helper website explains how to find out more.

If we realise our pensions will be insufficient, we can work longer. Working for perhaps five years longer and continuing to contribute to our pension pot can have a significant impact.

State pension

This is a popular session on the pre-retirement seminars I run. It's useful to check your national insurance contributions to ensure you have paid enough contributions, your retirement date, and how much your pension will be. I've been checking mine regularly just to make sure, as many of us were contracted out for years.

The state pension provides the main source of income for nearly half of pensioners. Currently over 12 million people are in receipt of this. We think of the state pension as 'our money' as we contribute through our national insurance, but the pension we receive isn't our money, it is funded by the current working population. At £110bn it is the largest item within the UK's £250bn welfare spend.

Once you reach state pension age, you have it for the rest of your life, with those who are in better health and living longer, receiving more. We all have an option to defer the start date in exchange for a bigger pension. The earliest age you can start receiving your pension depends on your date of birth. Currently the state pension age is 66 for both men and women. For those born after 5 April 1960, there will be a phased increase in state pension age to 67, and to 68 by 2046, and this date may be brought forward.

Currently the full new state pension is £203.85 a week (April 2023), usually paid every four weeks. You can request for it to be paid weekly, once you have received your first payment. You have to claim your pension, about three months beforehand, but we also have a choice: we can defer it by a year or more gaining 1 per cent for every nine weeks you defer, which is just under 5.8 per cent over a year, increasing your pension by £10.70 per week. But it is a gamble; we don't know how long we will live.

Pension credit

Pension credit is payable to top up a pensioners' income to a guaranteed minimum level of £201 or £307 for a couple (April 2023). It is worth checking your eligibility, as many people entitled to pension credit don't claim it. There is also help with council tax and heating and perhaps rent.

Are you caring for a grandchild or other relative?

Some of us will have given up work to look after an elderly relative or grandchild. If that's you, you can claim national insurance credits that could boost your state pension if you don't have the full 35 years. Each year short of 35 reduces the pay out by around £300 a year.

Alternatives ways of raising money, including claiming your state benefits

Chapter 5 covers different ways of earning money, and as the government is seeking more older people back into work, we should be able to get a job if we want to. Part-time working can meet many of our needs in addition to financial. Work in an office and you can happily work into your 70s, but it is different for those who have been manual workers all their lives.

You could consider downsizing, and, most importantly, make sure you are getting all the state benefits you are entitled to. Don't forget you currently stop paying national insurance contributions once you hit state retirement age.

... and spending less

When I look back on how much I was spending on holidays in my 50s ... Now I'm less interested in travelling the world and more interested in understanding me more. I'm selling possessions, recently selling my vinyl collection, and I buy less. Looking at the data behind having a comfortable retirement, it allowed for £1,300 to be spent on clothes. Looking back over the past year, I've spent nothing like that, but I have bought a chainsaw and other things for our woodland basecamp. All will last for years.

Activity 8.3

It's useful to create a plan of how much money you are spending now and what your spending will be like in retirement. Be realistic on where your money goes, and if it won't be enough, we need to get more money coming in or have less going out.

We can often be very cautious about sharing this information with others, so perhaps you want to talk in more general ways about how to reduce expenditure with your reflections buddy.

Inequality

Most people do not reach state pension age in good health. Only 30 per cent of women and 20 per cent of men are likely to reach the state pension age of 68 in good health and the lowest earners (who are often less well-educated and in poorer health) are more likely to die sooner.

There's a real difference between working in a physically demanding job and being able to work in a comfortable office. Whilst office workers can continue working beyond the state retirement age if they choose, those working in heavy jobs or on their feet all day are more likely to have to stop working earlier. These are also likely to be people who started work at 16.

This can lead to more inequality with those who are already in ill health.

Wills and LPAs

More than half of UK adults don't have a will, but it's the simplest way to legally specify what should happen to your assets after you're gone. As you approach retirement, updating or creating a will should be a priority. Dying intestate means your estate will be distributed according to laws that may not reflect your wishes.

There are two lasting powers of attorney (LPA). The property and financial affairs LPA protects your financial well-being if you become unable to make financial decisions for yourself. By appointing a trusted individual to manage your affairs, your chosen attorney can manage your finances, pay bills, and collect benefits on your behalf, giving you peace of mind knowing that your finances will be in good hands in the event of an accident or illness. There is also a health and welfare LPA, which covers your daily routine and medical care. Companies will encourage you to allow them to do it for you, at a cost of £500 upwards in addition to the LPA fees. This is something you could do yourself. I did it for my mum and got it right first time. The instructions are clear, you just follow them.

BEFORE YOU MOVE ON ...

As we end this chapter, I'd like you to consider these two questions:

1. Imagine that you are your future self. What would that person want you to know and do regarding how you spend money and what you save?
2. What one small step can you take today to spend less or save more?

You may like to write your answers in your journal and perhaps talk about this with your reflections buddy.

NOTE

1 Poterba, James M., Venti, Steven F., & Wise, David A. (1996). How retirement saving programs increase saving. *Journal of Economic Perspectives*, 10(4), 91–112.

PART 3

RENEW

Finding meaning and the new you in retirement

MEANING, MATTERING, AND GENERATIVITY

Why you should read this chapter

Throughout life people seek meaning to their existence, and retirement can be the trigger for people to focus on having more meaning in their lives and to review and reflect on their life to date, creating a new understanding of their life story. This chapter will guide you through an understanding of what we mean by meaning, how other people have found it, and what you can do next. Meaning and purpose are often considered interchangeably, but there is a difference, which will be discussed. Meaning includes a sense of 'do we matter?' We also look at happiness; there is nothing wrong with a focus on happiness, but we also need meaning in our lives.

REDIRECTION

We have talked about life transitions, reviewed our life to date, and now we are ready to move forward. We will look at meaning and purpose, mattering and generativity, taking an evidence-based approach. But let's start by a review of all the work done so far. I like the name for this phase being redirection.[1] There are four tasks involved in redirection: redefining, discovery, renewal, and integration.

Redefining involves seeing oneself in different ways than one did when working. We covered this in earlier chapters,

DOI: 10.4324/9781003374206-12

where you looked inside and also considered your new identity.

Discovery involves trying new things, joining new groups, and gathering information. You have explored options, looked to join groups, considered developing relationships, and also considered stepping outside your comfort zone.

Personal renewal occurs when a new path to meaning is found. This is the aim of this section. And then you will move to **integration**, resulting in a new sense of self and a new lifestyle.

And this could be an iterative process as people leave and return to the workplace. For future generations, and for some of us, retirement will no longer be a distinct life stage.

AM I RETIRED?

Whilst some may be reading this as they plan for retirement; others will already have moved into retirement. Whichever position you are in, it is worth thinking about the type of retirement you have or want and how you will describe it.

Most people in this book refer to themselves as semi-retired. Many people don't like the baggage that comes with the word 'retired', even when they no longer do paid work. Mary said that she would never call herself retired as she intended to remain active, even though it was unlikely to be paid work. Hilary saw being retired as being old and decrepit. "Of course I'll never be retired," she said. Vidhi was studying part-time and said, "I'm a student now, not retired!"

Continuity theory backs up the views of many. They continue in their professional work, with part-time work or as a consultant, sometimes setting up their own business. This helps to maintain their identity, allowing them to continue to use their skills. Others continue with part-time low-paid work at a local store, or continue their role as carer for elderly parents or their spouse, or care for grandchildren. So, little change.

For some, change is an important factor. They will move to something different. Others focus more on leisure and a traditional retirement. A third option is to reinvent ourselves and try something new. Kate left nursing to become a therapist and Gina started making cakes and chocolates instead of working in financial services. But not everyone has positive change. Ian had to retire due to ill health and Yvonne had to care for her husband who had been diagnosed with a degenerative disease. She was not having the retirement she had worked hard for. Julie caring for her elderly mother, saw it very much as her duty, and whilst she had planned to get involved in crafts, she had little free time as she continued as a carer.

What's coming up?

The following chapters use research interviews; I wanted to go beyond an academic analysis to understand the lived experience, how people make sense of their personal and social world. There are seven people – five female, two male – who had retired from full-time work within the last ten years; they self-identified as having found meaning at this stage of life and their 'story' made an interesting read. With seven people I could look at the subject in depth rather than relying on crunching numbers, as found in so much academic research.

The approach I took to my research was to focus on a homogenous group with shared aspects in common. Whilst all participants could be seen as 'WEIRD' – white, educated, industrialised, rich democracies[2] – this was not a conscious choice; but, on reflection, in the Western world it is easier to think about a meaningful life when you do not need to worry over earning enough to meet basic needs for accommodation, food, and heating. People from different cultures also can think differently about the world, and this has been shaped by their environment. There are clearly differences with those of us who live in the industrialised Global North compared to those in the developing world. This research did not seek to be inclusive, but it is worth noting that within different cultures, results could differ, and this leads back to the need to consider the impact on the individual.

The participants have sufficient financial resources to make the choice to retire from full-time work. We need to remember that not everyone has this freedom; other people need to stay working in a job that is unsatisfactory, purely for the income needed to meet bills, but we can still look for meaning in our life, despite our lack of funds.

Finding a sense of meaning, a purpose for life, to live to one's full potential,[3] was important to all. They wanted to move beyond being happy to feel their life has meaning, and this is seen as comparatively rare.[4] A sense of meaning is the general conviction that an individual is fulfilling a unique role or purpose in life, where we can live to our full potential as a human. For these participants, being curious relates to seeking meaning.[5] We can't know whether someone has meaning in life through observation, or an understanding of their personal circumstances; it is subjective and can only be ascertained through listening to them talk about their inner experience.[6]

MEANING AND PURPOSE (AND HAPPINESS)

A search for meaning

Throughout life, people seek meaning to their lives and I'm now going to guide you through an understanding of what we mean by meaning, how other people have found it, and what you can do next. Meaning and purpose are often considered interchangeably but there is a difference, and I'm going to take a considered view shortly. Meaning includes a sense of 'Do we matter?'

Did you get meaning through your work? People who have a calling – to teach, to heal, as an artist etc. – can see meaning through their work. Equally, you can find meaning in work that is more mundane; you can choose to find meaning as a cleaner or a delivery driver.

Meaning and happiness

Viktor Frankl, who wrote *Man's Search for Meaning*, said: "Happiness cannot be pursued, it must ensue. One must have a reason to be happy." And it is this meaning that leads to happiness. According to Martin Seligman,[7] there are three paths to happiness. The first is focused on short-term pleasures. The second is to get 'deeply involved in those activities in which one excels and losing oneself in the process'. The third is the meaningful life, where a person goes beyond the self and uses their strengths in the service of something that is bigger than they are.[8]

Research conducted by a team lead by psychologist Roy Baumeister[9] identified five factors that differentiate meaning and happiness.

1. Happiness is looking inwards, focused on what an individual wants, a life that is easy and satisfies wants and needs. Whereas meaning is focused outwards and having an impact on the wider world where we can contribute to the community or society. It can come with some struggles and challenges.
2. Happiness is closely tied to the present moment, whereas meaning is derived from weaving together the past, present, and future into a cohesive narrative. For instance, while achieving a promotion may provide an instant boost of happiness, some individuals may forego this momentary pleasure to pursue something that aligns with their long-term values and contributes to a bigger picture.
3. Establishing meaningful connections with others is crucial for both happiness and meaning, yet the nature of these connections shapes the type of fulfilment one derives from them. Baumeister's research indicates that aiding others contributes to a sense of meaning, whereas receiving assistance from others generates happiness.
4. Stress and struggles lead to a decline in happiness, but they contribute to a meaningful life.
5. We gain meaning when we can participate in activities that 'express the self' but this has little relevance to happiness.

There is nothing wrong with a focus on happiness; we all want to be happy and too many aren't, they have a negative view of life. We can be happy with the small things in life – an early morning coffee sat in the garden, listening to your grandchild read, your sports team winning, a hug with a friend, booking and anticipating a trip abroad. But as can be seen above, we also need meaning.

What is meaning?

Meaning and purpose are often used interchangeably; having looked at different definitions, I see having a purpose gives meaning to our life, and having meaning provides a sense of belonging, comprehension, and significance. It is where you make a difference, where your life is bigger than yourself.

"Meaning provides us with the sense that our lives matter, that they make sense, and that they are more than the sum of our seconds, days, and years."[10] This does not have to be at a 'change-the-world' level, but people need to feel that they have found a way that is meaningful for them.

Through much of our life to date, we may have been focused on doing – getting promoted, earning enough to pay the bills, dealing with all the stress we get as an adult. Our work has given us meaning and this meaning has given us our identity. If we can find meaning through our work, what about when we leave work? Part-time work may help with having meaning in life, but eventually a new way of finding meaning will need to be addressed as we finally retire.[11]

Meaning is not fixed but can change over time.[12] Although philosophers may say that definitions of a meaningful life are complex,[13,14] it is comprehensible, and characterised by regularity, predictability, or reliable connections with others.[15] Meaning refers to how people see their lives as being significant with a purpose or mission that drives them. Having an intention to accomplish something that is meaningful to the individual leads to an engagement with the world that is beyond the self,[16] so choosing to do something, with the motivation coming from within, can lead to meaning to the individual.

The term eudaimonia means flourishing and is the feeling that our life has meaning and that we are reaching our potential. People may feel that life is meaningful if they find it consistently rewarding in some way, even if they cannot articulate just what it all means.

Purpose

Having a purpose goes beyond mere busyness, as it involves feeling needed and appreciated. It entails recognising your talents, skills, and strengths, and finding ways to utilise them to benefit others and the world at large. This provides our lives with significance.

Having a sense of purpose can lead to a longer life. A study[17] tracked the physical and mental health of over 7,000 American adults aged 20 to 75 for 14 years. The study found that those who perceived a sense of direction or purpose in their lives lived longer than those who did not.

Activity 9.1

Journal: you've been completing a journal throughout this book; now is a good time to review it and pull out the times when you have felt fulfilled. What were you doing, who were you with, how deeply were you energised? It will help to continue journalling as you move forward.

Values-driven: you've identified your values, now check on how well you are living in line with them. How can you focus more on your values in your day-to-day life?

Relationships: it's less about you than other people; to what extent are you contributing to the well-being of others?

Make a note in your journal on these three areas.

Meaning beyond work - exploring meaning in retirement

Some people, making the adjustment into retirement, can see this as 20+ years when they can be what they have always wanted to be. Many young people are activists, they have freedom of thought, helped by not having many responsibilities. In mid-adulthood people are often weighed down by responsibility. As we move into later adulthood, some may reconnect with younger selves. To return to living in line with their values. Taking an active route rather than being passive. A time of greater meaning in life, to find their life purpose. To work towards a legacy, and to give back. In Western society we don't have a role of older people moving up to the role of elder which provides people with a purpose and meaning, whereas this is more common in Indigenous societies, such as the Agìkùyù and the Samburu of Kenya.[18]

The experience of retirement can be the trigger for people to seek meaning in their lives and to review their life journey; to create a new understanding of their life story;[19] a time for reflection on their life to date and a sense of where their life is heading. This can lead people to revise the direction of their life with a consideration of life priorities, values, and future goals.[20]

Whilst for some, retirement is a time to sit back and do nothing, it is not the goal of everyone, and certainly not for the people I interviewed. In wider society, many people do not find that a life of recreational activities such as daily golf, coffee and chats, and regular trips away provides long-term meaning. For a meaningful life, we need a sense of purpose, our reason to get up in the morning. We need the self-belief that we can make a difference and it allows us to be authentically who we are. It also needs good connections with other people.

Considering one's life to be meaningful is associated with higher quality of life, superior self-reported health,[21] and decreased mortality.[22,23] It predicts slower age-related cognitive decline and decreased risk for Alzheimer's disease.[24]

A loss of purpose

Many new retirees had purpose through their work. Retirement starts as an extended holiday with days out, looking after grandchildren, decorating, playing golf, and travel. They talk about being busy and wonder how they ever had time for work, but the focus is on short-term pleasure. The purpose from work has gone, whether it be a satisfying job, or money to pay the bills; there was reason for going to work each day. We spoke in Chapter 5 about continuing to work and other ways to fill this gap such as volunteering, study, and satisfying pursuits.

Once people retire, there is a loss of status from the job, and also the loss of the meaning and purpose that has been gained from their work.[25,26] Many retired people report feeling a sense of emptiness and loss of meaning in this phase of life.[27] This loss of life's meaning can lead to a loss of self-esteem and an impact on overall health, and our mental health can suffer from a lack of direction and stimulation.

We can find purpose and fulfilment in retirement through continuing with some work, learning new things, being curious, and by mentoring, teaching, or volunteering. We can also find purpose in small moments of our life. Viktor Frankl[28] wrote about how, when in a concentration camp, if he could say a kind word, give someone a crust of bread, or give someone a hug, these things made his life more meaningful and helped him to get through another day. For us this can be by being a good listener, a good friend, a sounding board to others where we don't try and solve things for them.

Activity 9.2

Let's consider the meaning and purpose in your life. With the questions below, indicate if they are not true, partly true, mainly true or fully true.

	Not true	Partly true	Mainly true	Fully true
I understand what makes my life meaningful.				
I have a clear purpose to my life.				
I feel part of something that is bigger than me.				
I lead a fulfilled life.				
There is a deeper meaning to my life.				
My life feels significant.				
I have found my life's purpose.				
I remain curious for further direction to my life.				
I have a belief in the divine – spiritual or religious faith.				

High scores on each of these questions means that your life has purpose and probably you are open to exploring things further.

You are likely to be content with your life and optimistic for the future. Low scores are likely to mean that you don't feel as if your life has a significant purpose or meaning, and you're not actively seeking or exploring ways to find that meaning. You may experience dissatisfaction with your life or yourself, and you may not feel particularly optimistic about the future. If you relate more to the latter, are there some action steps you would like to take?

FINDING YOUR PURPOSE

We spoke earlier about how we have gained an extra 30 years of life compared to a couple of generations ago. These extra years are added to now, not to the end of our life. We can use these years to live a purposeful life that will also make us happier and healthier. If your sense of purpose is unclear, now is a good time to identify it.

A good way to find your purpose is to focus on how to grow and give. It's less about having goals, and more about how you can develop more as a person and how you can give to the world.

Ikigai

The Japanese define purpose with the concept of Ikigai (pronounced ee-kee-guy). It's essentially the reason why we get up in the morning. The Westernised version of Ikigai has four components and is the intersection of what you love, what you are good at, what the world needs, and what you can get paid for. In Japan, it is less about income and doesn't have to be around work. It's more to do with small joys in everyday life rather than our big life purpose and feeling that what we do makes a difference to the lives of others. This fits well with us in retirement, where getting paid may not be as relevant; it's the joy we get through being appreciated and valued. Let's look at these four components:

1. What you love

Do you know what you love? It's worth taking some time to identify your passions, the things you truly care about. The things that make you lose track of time. One way to identify your passions is to reflect on the proudest moments in your life and unpack the motivators, values, interests, and skills that drove those accomplishments. By recognising the activities that bring pleasure and fulfilment, you may uncover a potential passion.

You can also journal using questions such as: 'When you look back on your life at 90, what were your greatest contributions to the world?' 'If you had the means to pursue your dream job, what activities would you be doing?' 'What would the environment and colleagues be like?' 'If you asked five friends to describe your gifts and talents, what would they say?' 'If you could live someone else's life for a week, who would you choose, and why?' You can also consider the things that excite you, outside of work – playing the guitar, visiting an art gallery, a quiet walk alone in the natural world or the camaraderie of being at a large sporting or music event.

2. What you are good at

You have already looked at your career history in Chapter 5; you can also find out about your character/signature strengths such as using the activity on the www.viacharacter.org website. Get clear not only on the things that you are good at, but the things you want to continue to do. You can involve others with this stage too, such as by asking friends and colleagues to share examples (stories) of when you have been at your best. You can do it for others too. This helps us all to focus on our 'best possible selves' (more on this in Chapter 13).

3. What the world needs

Take time to research what is needed, whether it is in the wider world, your community, or an employer. You can read the business press, look at occupational growth via the Future Jobs Reports from the World Economic Forum, and check out LinkedIn for details on the fastest-growing jobs in the world. You can then get more depth through fact-finding interviews.

4. What you can get paid for

Whilst money is often a key priority when younger, in this later stage of life a big salary may not be the main driver, but we may still want to feel valued and have recognition for the work we do. So, we may want to find out if we can make money from it?

Activity 9.3

Consider your current life; to what extent does this provide you with meaning? If you can't think of a reason, can you break your job down into components; what part of your job brings you alive. Marcia worked in retail management and was bored and frustrated with the focus on targets. Talking with her, it was the calming down of an irate customer that was the most satisfying part of her job, and this led her to work in a prison after retirement, helping prisoners to improve their communication skills. If you can't wait to retire to leave your job, could this help you to improve things for now?

You can also look again at your values and see to what extent your life is consistent with them.

MATTERING

The term 'mattering' was coined by Rosenberg and McCullough.[29] They found that "The problem of retirement is that one no longer matters; others no longer depend upon [retirees]. The reward of retirement [may] be the punishment of not mattering." Knowing that you 'matter' is important at any stage of life, but it becomes more important (to most people) when you retire. At retirement, some of the things that have given you a sense that you matter, particularly your job, are gone. Retirement can leave us feeling disconnected from former colleagues who carry on without us, and when our children have grown what they want from us has changed and we can feel a bit lost with an empty nest.

While we may try to ignore these feelings for a time, eventually we are faced with the reality of our changing role in the world. Feeling relevant is what keeps us connected and makes us feel like we are making a difference – both to ourselves and to others; feeling irrelevant can leave us questioning our value and importance in the world. We can feel invisible and unrecognised.

With less-formal work roles, relationships with others increases in importance and lead to stronger feelings of mattering. Mattering helps to increase our well-being in retirement alongside our work and relationships. From both, we get feedback that we matter and when we lose the work role it needs to be filled in some way. Retirement is a big transition, and understanding what matters for your well-being before retirement can help you adjust and thrive during retirement. It's important to understand how your life and retirement projects matter to yourself and to others.

Family and friends provide a sense of mattering. In the workplace, it's easy to know you matter because of specific tasks and responsibilities. Outside of work, connections with friends and family can give you a sense of purpose and enhance your quality of life.

Volunteering and helping others can provide personal satisfaction, make you feel valued and needed, and enhance your sense of mattering. It's a way to make a difference and contribute to the lives of others. Caregiving, whilst important, has less of an impact on whether we feel that we matter, or not.[30] This could be because volunteering typically occurs within a structured organisation or association that has specific objectives and targets, whereas caregiving activities are typically more informal, as they involve looking after family members and loved ones.[31] This type of care may only be acknowledged by a limited social network, which can result in a diminished perception of mattering as a social contribution.

Identifying the skills that you have developed so far and finding ways to use them in practical ways can provide a sense of purpose and fulfilment and can help show that you matter. This could be through using your skills and experience to be a mentor to others. Additionally, learning something new, such as pursuing higher education or developing a new hobby, can give you a sense of growth and accomplishment.

Activity 9.4

None of my clients had ever considered if they matter; answering these questions made them stop and think. I'd like you to do the same. Rate yourself against these questions and then journal your thoughts.

	Not at all	A little	Some-what	A lot
How much do people depend on you?				
How much do people pay attention to you? By listening to what you say?				
To what extent would you be missed if you weren't here?				
Are people interested in what you have to say?				
Do people like having you around?				

Actions you could take

If overall you have said that you do matter, then you may not need to take any further action. If you say no – what is it that you can do to make you feel that you do matter? Something to reflect and journal on.

GENERATIVITY

I introduced you to generativity in Chapter 5. Generativity is one of Erikson's eight stages of psychosocial development. Before we reach the final stage with the wisdom virtue (ego integrity vs. despair) we are at the generativity vs stagnation stage with a basic virtue of care.[32] It's a useful model to use as we consider the challenges we face at this age.

Generativity is an integral component of the healthy adult personality and consists of both social and individual factors. It is around making our mark on the world, creating or nurturing things that will live on beyond us. Without this, we can feel stagnant and unproductive and perhaps disconnected with our community and wider society. Generativity[33] is positively associated with adjustment; and highly generative individuals may be able to sustain a sense of meaning and contribution to larger purposes once they enter retirement.

As well as helping us to matter, volunteering and socially useful work is a way of experiencing generativity. Our motives with this tend to differ with age; now it is less about what is in it for us, such as developing skills to enhance our career, and more about giving back. A study of American seniors[34] reported that the three most frequent reasons for volunteering were to 'help others' (83%), 'to feel useful or productive' (65%), and 'to fulfil a moral responsibility' (51%). When compared to others, those who chose 'feeling useful or productive' as the main reason were over four times more likely to volunteer two or more times a month.

Highly generative adults tend to be enthusiastic, expansive, and self-confident people, who are actively assertive, and demonstrate positive emotions. They are more likely to have a sense of duty and self-discipline. They are productive, with a focus on achievement, caring with warmth, trust, and altruism, wanting to make a positive difference in the world. Lots of positive qualities there! If you don't see how you match up, there are ways to become more trusting etc. Personality is not fixed.

Positive emotions can promote social connections and lead to productive and caring commitments that are routed in generativity. When we are anxious or sad, we are less likely to focus on generativity, and if that is you, it's worth getting support in this area.

Activity 9.5

I've identified 11 areas that relate to generativity. Consider each of the questions below and decide to what extent these are things you can agree with. You can be truthful; this is only for you unless you choose to share with your reflections buddy.

	Never	Some-times	Often
People say I have a positive effect on others.			
I feel as though I have made a difference to many people.			
I feel needed by other people.			
People come to me for advice.			
I feel I will leave things behind that will live on when I am gone.			
I have important skills that I try to teach others.			
People say I am a very productive person.			
I believe society should take responsibility for those in need.			
I see myself as a role model to younger people.			
I volunteer for a charity.			
I try to pass along the knowledge I have gained through my experiences.			

As you look at your scores you may feel happy with what you are doing, or it may give you some suggestions for things you can do. When we are focused on our work this is not something we may have considered, but now could be a good time to think about our impact on the wider world.

Make a note in your journal of a couple of things you would like to do after completing this exercise.

ONE LAST THING BEFORE YOU MOVE ON …

Meaning is so important to us at all life stages, especially in later life. You have reflected on meaning and mattering and considered how to get more purpose to your life. It's helpful to review this and see how much clarity you can have on your purpose for the future. I suggest you journal on this and discuss with your reflections buddy. If you are still unsure, the next three chapters, where we are going to look deep into three areas – search for knowledge, a change in 'time', and who I am – will help.

NOTES

1 Cook, S.L. (2015). Redirection: An extension of career during retirement. *The Gerontologist*, 55(3), 360–373.

2 Henrich, J., Heine, S. J., & Norenzayan, A. (2010). The weirdest people in the world? *Behavioral and Brain Sciences*, 33, 61–83.

3 Breitbart, W., (2002). Spirituality and meaning in supportive care: spirituality and meaning centered group psychotherapy interventions in advanced cancer. *Supportive Care in Cancer*, 10(4), 272–280.

4 Sligman, M.E.P. (2011). *Flourish: A Visionary New Understanding of Happiness and Well-Being*. Free Press, New York.

5 Breitbart, Spirituality and meaning in supportive care.

6 Heintzelman, S.J., & King, L.A. (2014). Life is pretty meaningful. *American Psychologist*, 69(6), 561-574.

7 Seligman, M.E.P. (2002). *Authentic Happiness: Using the New Positive Psychology to Realize Your Potential for Lasting Fulfillment*. London: Nicholas Brealey.

8 Cotton Bronk, K., Hill, P.L., Lapsley, D.K., Talib, T.L., & Finch, H. (2009). Purpose, hope, and life satisfaction in three age groups. *The Journal of Positive Psychology*, 4(6), 500–510.

9 Baumeister, R. F., & Vohs, K. D. (2002). The pursuit of meaningfulness in life. In C. R. Snyder & S. J. Lopez (Eds.), *Handbook of Positive Psychology* (608–618). Oxford University Press.

10 Steger, M.F. (2009). Meaning in life. In S.J. Lopez & C.R. Snyder (Eds.), *Oxford Handbook of Positive Psychology* (679–687). Oxford University Press, Oxford.

11 Matour, S., & Prout, M.F. (2007). Psychological implications of retirement in the 21st century. *Journal of Financial Service Professionals*, 57–64.

12 Bengtsson, M., & Flisbäck, M. (2021). Existential driving forces to work after retirement: The example of physicians' mentoring. *Nordic Journal of Working Life Studies*.

13 Baumeister, R.F. (1991). *Meanings of Life*. Guilford Press.

14 Audi R. (2005). Intrinsic value and meaningful life. *Philosophical Papers*, 34(3), 331–355.

15 Antonovsky, A. (1993). The structure and properties of the sense of coherence scale. *Social Science & Medicine*, 36(6), 125–733.

16 Damon, W., Menon, J., & Bronk, K.C. (2003). The development of purpose during adolescence. *Applied Developmental Science, 7*, 119–128.

17 Hill, P.L., & Turiano, N.A. (2014). Purpose in life as a predictor of mortality across adulthood. *Psychological Science*, 25(7), 1482–1486.

18 Mutua, A.F. (2014). Accessed on 12 May 2021 https://afrikancounselofelders.wordpress.com/2014/05/16/elders-as-peacemakers/

19 McAdams, D. P. (2001). The psychology of life stories. *Review of General Psychology*, 5, 100–122.

20 Amabile, T. (2019). Understanding retirement requires getting inside people's stories: A call for more qualitative research work. *Aging and Retirement*, 5(3), 207–211.

21 Steger, Meaning in life. In *Oxford Handbook of Positive Psychology*.

22 Krause, N. (2009). Meaning in life and mortality. *Journals of Gerontology: Series B: Psychological Sciences and Social Sciences*, 64B, 517–527.

23 Boyle, P. A., Barnes, L. L., Buchman, A. S., & Bennett, D. A. (2009). Purpose in life is associated with mortality among community-dwelling older persons. *Psychosomatic Medicine*, 71, 574–579.

24 Ibid.

25 Reis, M., & Gold, D.P. (1993). Retirement, personality, and life satisfaction: A review and two models. *The Journal of Applied Gerontology*, 12, 261–282.

26 Wang, M., & Shi, J. (2014). Psychological research on retirement. *Annual Review of Psychology*, 65, 209–233.

27 Jonsson H., Borell L., & Sadlo G., (2000): Retirement: An occupational transition with consequences for temporality, balance and meaning of occupations, *Journal of Occupational Science*, 7(1), 29-37.

28 Frankl, V. (1959). *Man's Search for Meaning*. Beacon Press, Boston, MA.

29 Rosenberg, M., & McCullough, B. (1981). Mattering: Inferred significance and mental health among adolescents. *Research in Community & Mental Health*, 2, 163–182.

30 Froidevaux, A., Hirsch, A., & Wang. M., (2016). The role of mattering as an overlooked key challenge in retirement planning and adjustment. *Journal of Vocational Behavior*, 94, 57–69.

31 Blustein, D.L. (2011). A relational theory of working. *Journal of Vocational Behavior*, 79(1), 1–17.

32 Erikson, E.H. (1963). *Childhood and Society* (2nd ed.). Norton, New York.

33 Serrat, R., Villar, F., Pratt, M.W., & Stukas A.A. (2018). On the quality of adjustment to retirement: The longitudinal role of personality traits and generativity. *Journal of Personality*, 86(3), 435–449.

34 Okun, M.A. (1994). The relation between motives for organizational volunteering and frequency of volunteering by elders. *Journal of Applied Gerontology*, 13, 115–126.

10

SEARCH FOR KNOWLEDGE

Why you should read this chapter

In this chapter you get to read and learn from the stories of the people I interviewed. It covers a search for knowledge at different life stages and includes being curious, where people are looking for new things; earlier stages in life; the need to look inside ourselves; and how our search for knowledge changes as we move into retirement. This ties in with mastery and motivation.

I've included a number of activities to get you to reflect on specific areas. As we reach the end, I'll be asking you to write a story about your search for knowledge, both looking back to your past and towards your future. There may be other details that resonate, so even if there isn't a specific activity, feel free to pause and make a note in your journal and perhaps discuss with your reflections buddy.

At this later stage in life, a loss of meaning through work can lead to older adults looking for meaning in their life through the pursuit of significant activities. We can continue with existing approaches or opt for something new. We learn and gather ideas through conversations with others, so read on for inspiration from seven remarkable yet ordinary people.

BEING CURIOUS

Part of knowledge exploration is to be curious, mentioned by everyone. Being curious relates to aliveness and this aliveness

DOI: 10.4324/9781003374206-13

gives life meaning. Without meaning, what is life about? Without curiosity, it is about stagnation. Arthur said "I have to have this constant flow of new things going into my eyes, into my ears, to stimulate my brain. I love it. And if I don't get it. I seek it out. Because I know I need it. If I didn't, I would vegetate, I would become bored. And there's no way that's gonna happen. I've got too much life left in me."

Arthur is very alert to his senses, with reference to his eyes and ears; it is about what he hears and sees. Saying that he will not vegetate, he will avoid living in a dull, inactive, and unchallenging way. Instead, he seeks new things out; he is proactive, not waiting to see what comes into view. He needs new things, they are part of who he is; he's not going to get bored, there is "no way that's gonna happen", more evidence of being proactive and taking control. There's too much life left – he is not in a 'waiting room' to the end of his life but seeking an aliveness within.

> It is worth paying attention to all of your senses, not just what you think. To move away from your logical brain to notice what you can see, hear, and how it makes you feel.

Sometimes curiosity was referred to early on in an interview, Claire said: "I've never shied away from switching and doing things differently, learning new things, that type of thing. And I think I've always been quite curious." She recognised the trait of curiosity, which continued from earlier times. Again proactive, she won't 'shy away', but seeks things out and takes her own approach. Doing things differently suggests that she is assertive enough, and comfortable in her own skin, to do things her way, seeking to understand more and to find things that are meaningful.

Sally said that one of the themes of her life was being inquisitive and how this has defined everything. "Inquisitiveness came into all of my ... I think it's just weaved in my whole life and what I read." For Sally and others, they can have a trait of curiosity as a lens to see the world and to use this to find out more, to explore and expand their thinking. It can be seen as part of who we are. This is around seeking meaning, as through the process of finding out new things, it can make one feel alive. "I'm always trying to figure out, doing something to keep my hand in the climate world." Not content to just take things at a surface level, but to 'figure it out', to dig deeper, to understand more about the purpose of the work she does; and having a purpose is an important aspect of being alive. This is pursued by Sally as she moves into retirement.

Sally remains curious on how her life will unfold "One of the themes of my retirement is, I'm super open-minded to stuff and in a way the pandemic has been good because there's all these learning opportunities now. I take individual classes or a smaller short series." The search for meaning is never ending and she is putting pressure on herself to find her place. Being "super open-minded" is quite a strong description and can reflect how she sees herself. Her self-identity is being proactive to take advantage of "all these learning opportunities"; she is seeing the positive from the COVID-19 pandemic.

Activity 10.1

Being curious will open ourselves to the new, to exploring more, and finding things out. Make a note in your journal of recent times when you have been curious. If nothing recent comes to mind, look further back and also make a note of any reason why you haven't followed a path of curiosity. Is this something you would like to develop?

Being Proactive

Arthur, Claire, and Sally have proactive personalities. They see retirement as a new challenge. Being proactive led Doug to set up a music festival and Helen to consider a PhD. The participants also showed themselves as having qualities of the 'enterprising self'.[1]

> **Activity 10.2**
>
> Look back at Chapter 4 where we considered the proactive personality. Make a note of how you have been, and currently are, proactive. How have you taken control of life decisions? Of course, this may not be a strength of yours. If that is so, you may like to journal around the reasons for this, looking back at your earlier life experiences.

Still searching

Sally had come to the interview as someone who said she had found meaning in life, but as the conversation unfolded, I became more aware of it being a process that she is experiencing now. "I'm constantly thinking about where I want to be in this world. ... I think it's more for me because I was in my 50s when I left the work world." Constantly thinking means it is at the forefront of her mind and something she is searching for. She is aware of her age, feeling that she is too young to just accept the situation; she needs to invest time and energy in where she is heading, seeking a passion and to find her place in the world. We all benefit from investing time, and reading this book, and the stories, will help you to make sense of where you are going.

It was a feeling

Claire had been seeking meaning in life after her full-time work, and curiosity for her was to recognise the strong feelings she got inside when she put her hands on someone, leading to her to study Reiki. "I suddenly had this really strong urge to go and put my hands near her ... so, I put my hands on, and I was sort of just instinctively putting hands around her head. ... so, I went and did a Reiki course, and this is weird, I can feel energy." This was instinctive. She was drawn to do something, maybe from deeper within her consciousness. Driven by a really strong urge, it sounds like this was something she had not been expecting; this had a strong impact, a sense of this could be it, maybe I have found what I should do, how I can give back to others. It felt weird to Claire that she could feel the energy.

***

Activity 10.3

Have you ever felt drawn to something with no real idea where it came from? Sometimes people have these glimpses into a future, based on their senses; they get an image or a feeling, but we are taught to ignore this type of knowing. Perhaps you may like to be more open to this. One way is when you are not thinking but just allowing yourself to be. Make a note on this in your journal.

***

Constantly new

If you are so curious that you don't want to experience the same thing twice, how does this affect a search for meaning? Is meaning going to be around new things and a constant exploration, never being satisfied with what one has, or is this part of the process, looking for new things and then choosing to settle into something new? This was the view of Sarah: "I've always been very curious and always wanted new experiences, and I'm very much still that way. I won't read a book twice, watch a movie twice, it has to be new." Always wanting a new experience is a strong way of describing this, and the examples were quite mundane, but so is much of life. If you want to experience new things at this level, the feeling to explore the new is likely to be stronger with the more important things that have a stronger impact on one's life.

CHILDHOOD AND ADULTHOOD

Being curious can show itself from childhood and early adulthood. Sarah spoke about adventures with her boyfriend on leaving school and early married life travelling around America. "It was amazing, because I was just a small-town girl and the thing that impressed me the most was everywhere we went whether it was a small town in Indiana, or Salt Lake City, wherever, we met other people who are just like us. They were just people and up until that it was an unknown." Using the word 'amazing', suggests the wonder of a child, and the recognition that people from different parts of America are "just like us" gave her a wider perspective than when in her hometown. It opened her eyes, broadened her horizon. Whilst she was happy to be seen as curious, when I said this was adventurous, she wasn't sure, saying "I don't jump out of aeroplanes." People have their own interpretation and can take a word such as 'adventurous' and see it and use it in different ways.

With Helen, curiosity underpinned much of her life, taking on a range of courses when her children where young, including reaching grade seven in singing and completing a law degree. She had a need to be actively learning and finding out more. "I've always studied … I went back to night school. I'm a qualified electrician, I have a level seven in music singing … and of course, running the companies that I ran, and the Civic Society kept me occupied. I just thought, what am I going to do now. So, I went to university." Helen is finding meaning through knowledge, and gaining qualifications is part of her identity; it defines her, and it appears she would be lost without this part of her life. For her, it was important to keep busy, to have a full life. As a child, she was brought up to be busy, perhaps with 'the devil makes work for idle hands' as part of her childhood, and with an ethically strong upbringing. Not knowing what to do next, she focuses on action, on doing, and whilst still focused on doing things in her retirement she is now taking time 'just to be'.

Activity 10.4

Take some time to reflect on your earlier life. What are some of the strongest memories that you have? How have they made you the person you are now? Some may be positive, others you have learned and developed from. They have all impacted on you today. Write them down in your journal.

Curiosity awakened

Curiosity is not always spoken about from earlier times. For Arthur, it was late-developing relationships that led to travel and a developing interest in other countries and cultures. "I went to a lot of different places, I started taking holidays for the first time in my life, slightly late in life, admittedly ... and my social life, a good social life, which included music, theatre, and so on continued to expand." For Arthur, curiosity seems to have lain dormant in his earlier adulthood but significant change in his personal life was the catalyst he needed to explore.

Doug talked about the adventures gained through his work, with world travel since age 21 and a deep interest in the studies that underpinned his work. "I really have had adventures through my professional activities, and an interest, personal interest that took me around the world multiple times. So, I've been a world traveller since I was 21." His words, seeing much of what he does as adventures, suggest an openness to the new, and a playful approach to work, seeking things out and embracing opportunities. The boundary between work and non-work is not always clear; with so much interest in exploration related to his work, it was less a part of his non-work conversation. With Doug it appears that being curious is part of his work identity, but his wider identity seems driven by this.

Enthusiasm in the workplace

Knowledge exploration can be helpful in the workplace, Arthur was successful at work because of a different world view to people who entered his field of expertise from a more mainstream perspective. This work was meaningful to him, and having now found it, it was something to seek in life after full-time work. "Amongst one of the things that I wanted to do was set up industry seminars and public-facing events. And I did that with huge enthusiasm. The enthusiasm wasn't always shared by my colleagues, sadly, but I kept going at it. I made my presence very much felt to our business and social enterprise partners." He spoke about his "huge enthusiasm", an excitement for things, and resilience to keep going, to not be disillusioned by the more negative response of others. Having enthusiasm can drive us to seek out positive experiences and provide us with a real passion for activity, which comes later in his new interest in photographing bands.

Activity 10.5

In this activity I would like you to focus on you at work. Reading the stories of Doug and Arthur, and their openness and enthusiasm from their work, does this suggest anything for you to reflect on and write in your journal?

FROM WITHIN

Spirituality and introspection

Curiosity is not only with the world outside but can also be within. Several of the participants spoke about spirituality, with an interest in Eastern methodologies, mindfulness, and meditation. Doug's example was reasonably typical: "I have had these interests in Eastern, and other spiritual paths for years, and certainly in my leisure time. I get to be quiet and introspective and do mindfulness practices." Mindfulness and meditation allow for quiet and introspection, time away from a busy life, to close down the chatter in our head, to ponder and reflect on life, our thoughts, and experiences; whilst talk of religion was rarely covered, broader spirituality was.

Introspection was also important to Sarah; it had a spiritual element, connecting to a higher self. "The preservation of my sanity probably has been having a spiritual life. I'm not a religious person, but I do love meditation, I do believe in connecting to a higher self, pursued via meditation and yoga practice and journalling." When Sarah talks about the "preservation of my sanity" it suggests a strong pull on her being. It is something that she has to do. Meaning is not just something that we find out there, but also what we can find inside us.

Activity 10.6

To what extent do you class yourself as spiritual? It may be an organised religion, or something else. How does this help you have meaning in your life? You may like to write some notes in your journal.

Authenticity and nature

Spirituality has a connectedness to authenticity.[2] Authenticity is seen as filling a 'spiritual void' in our modern world. Studies[3,] have focused on how inner development and spiritual growth, such as meditating, can lead to people to have a more authentic and fulfilled life. Tornstam's gerotranscendence theory[4] states that in later life we can connect more to this deeper, original self, and this leads to wisdom as we stop focusing on material possessions.

Whilst several took an Eastern view, with Claire it was to consider the 'old ways' of our culture: "I'd probably say I was a pagan … I believe in the power of the earth. I believe that there's energy and all of that sort of stuff." A belief in the power of the earth, to rekindle how our culture used to be; the shared energy that exists between people, like how trees communicate; the way that society used to have meaning, before the takeover of organised religion – there is a renaissance in later life of people connecting with nature and gaining wisdom from the natural world.

Having a belief can help people with a wider purpose in life and many mentioned nature alongside the spiritual side, like Doug: "My relationship with nature and spirituality and the regional environment is a big part of my gratification for having moved out west". For Doug, his interest in spiritual matters helps give him meaning, seeing this as being part of the wider world. It is also a deeper understanding of the self, getting to know who we are. This can be from early times in our lives, not just at this transition. Being reflective and thinking about what we have learned from the past is all part of knowledge-gathering and allows us to attribute meaning now based on our past.

> **Activity 10.7**
>
> How important is authenticity to you? Is it one of your values? To what extent did this value show up in the workplace? Can you now be authentic in your life? If not, and it is important to you, what is holding you back? Consider, too, time you spend in nature. Do you feel connected to the natural world? Feeling soil in our hands through gardening or walking barefoot across a meadow is a way to be grounded in nature. Take some time to reflect on this in your journal.

Work

Doug spoke about his university experience with experiential learning, including dream reflections to enable self-understanding and spiritual growth. "I started a dream seminar business in Seattle, Washington. And I had this university extension programme. Once I got to graduate school in Seattle for ten years I ran dream workshops, as an experiential leader of adult learning." He saw this introspection as part of his self-development; saying this is at the core of his being, who he really is, and something that has a significant impact on his life. In finding a purpose and understanding our place in the world we need to understand who we are. This can then be used in the workplace, like Doug did, and in our life after full-time work.

Travel

Rose spoke about taking time to get to know herself through solo travel. "I did a solo around the world trip. … that was transformative really, getting comfortable and spending time with just me." She spoke about it being transformative, a word with high impact; this is a time of change, like crossing a threshold into some new way of being, finding out what was important to her. It is around a radical and typically positive change. With Rose, this was taking an external event, the travel, and this led to having a deep change within her. She needed a 'time out' to find this.

Finding internal equilibrium

Rose also recognised the need to understand herself as a pre-requisite to finding meaning. "It showed up in every area, I felt misaligned in my marriage, in my body, in my career, in my social life, everything just felt out of whack." Feeling "misaligned" was also a way of finding her inner being; to make sure that her inside and outside were congruent. Saying how things "felt out of whack" is a strong pull to do something different and find equilibrium. She was able to find the alignment that brought her into balance. "That's what gave me meaning. During the first aspect of this new life. It was an internal meaning, and it was about aligning, it was about finding that alignment that I could tell was missing in the past." This resonated with me, who has been described as blossoming since the end of my marriage, finding the me that was hidden from years of marriage. Arthur, too, saw the end of a long-term relationship as a time to be free to explore and to make his own mistakes.

Activity 10.8

Travel is a great way to find out more about the person you are. You may like to journal about any experiences around solo travel or plans to do this. It can be via small-group holidays, or it can be where you travel solo. I found the latter option a wonderful way to get to know people and find an inner resource I didn't know I had. You can also find out more about who you are through time alone in nature.

Journalling

A reason for asking you to start a journal at the start of this book was learning how helpful other people have found it. Self-reflection can be helped by journalling, a technique practised by Sarah and Doug, both starting this many years ago. It provides an opportunity to reflect on thoughts and life events, and to use this for inner growth. "I've been journalling for 35 years. I have two journals going right back that are continuing with introspection and self-learning. In addition to 'Who am I?', a key question is, 'Who am I going to be next?' So, it's, that's becoming a story I would say that sustains me and is a source of meaning, where I'm continuing to inquire on the page and in dialogue with."

Doug has reflected on meaning and the journalling, and the 'dialogue with the page' allows him to go back and reflect on the past. Seeking to find out who we are going to be next is an important question, and will help to plan for the future, on activities that resonate and allow Doug to live a life with meaning. Journalling, and reflection, involve self-questioning, considering things carefully internally, and self-change, where changes can be made and presented to the outside world.

INTO RETIREMENT

Learning new

As the participants moved to retirement, they still had a passion for learning. Several participants saw this as a time to be open-minded and to expand knowledge, not to sit still. It could be taking advantage of the myriad of online courses due to COVID-19, as discussed by Sally. For Sally it was also learning more about her new interest in angel investing. "I found out about two of these angel investing networks, and I kind of explored both of them and I joined one of them, so I'm just starting." She had been seeking meaning, and this new activity gave her a sense of purpose and the chance to learn something new. She began with exploration, finding out more, and then deciding. It is still in the early stages, but is this what will give her meaning? She seems to still be looking, recognising she is just starting, but is this something she feels she ought to do? There was a drop in passion and enthusiasm with both her words and voice tone.

Knowledge exploration can also be more about being fearless and taking a risk in life. For Arthur, this showed itself through extensive travel, and a desire to see new things: "I have to have this constant flow of new things going into my eyes into my ears to stimulate my brain. I love it." But it is not only travel. Arthur wants to learn for the sake of learning, for his own self-satisfaction. He's pursuing new hobbies and interests that involve learning. Learning had been something he had pursued through his life; it was part of who he was. "It was primarily work-related, but I've just been like a sponge for learning all my life." He has been "like a sponge", eager to learn, but it has to be on his terms. In another part of the interview, he said he was disengaged when at school, so the learning seems to tie in with what he wants to do; he has control over what he learns and seeks mastery of a topic.

Retirement allowed Arthur to continue to learn, and part of this was expanding his interest in photography, to encompass the natural world, sport, and live music – very different to how he had done photography before. "I like to learn. Sometimes for the sake of learning. Not that I'll be using it for anything except my own self-satisfaction that I know this, I know how things work." To be able to study for "my own self-satisfaction", to learn for its own sake, to choose a topic because of interest and passion, is part of the freedom that comes when you can do what you want, and is important to Arthur.

Intellectual impact

Doug talked about intellectual discussions with smart friends, now in retirement, still having intellectual curiosity, keeping his brain active. "I still have energy for intellectual curiosity. And these relationships with the smart people that I've known in my life that are long term friends, satisfy and gratify." Is he putting himself under pressure? He wants to keep up with the smart people, so he is treating this as a challenge. However, with his smart friends, what happens if his brain became less sharp; would they remain part of his friendship group? Recognising that he still has energy, that he can still keep up, implies that he still feels valuable.

Research

Study and knowledge-gathering is part of how people find meaning in life after work, keeping brains active, demonstrating purpose, and giving structure to a day. For Helen, retirement was a time to remain curious about history, with more time to spend on this life-time passion. She was looking deep, with the possibility of doing a PhD. "I want to continue to go to these lectures with John Hunt, I'm still toying with the idea of doing a PhD. I still am, although what subject I would do it on I don't know." It looks like it is being considered but perhaps not strongly, as she is "toying with the idea"; there is no certainty to an action. Perhaps with her published articles, that is enough; she is known as a historian, the academic credentials may not be needed.

We spoke in the last chapter about how many people in retirement feel that they no longer matter, so the transition into retirement was helped by having things to do – either planned for in advance, such as Arthur and his focus on photography and writing; or developing in retirement, such as Sally with angel investing and Doug setting up a music festival. Mattering includes the impact to wider society. Later we read of Rose mentoring young people in Columbia and Helen leading historical talks. We see evidence of self-determined motivation throughout the interviews,[5] where the participants can have autonomy and freedom and participate in activities they want to do, which brings pleasure.

Activity 10.9

We spoke about learning new things in Chapter 5. Have you plans on things to learn? It's useful to create a list so you can decide what to do and it helps to have some variety. For James, it is to learn a language, develop his woodland management skills, and improve his computer skills. Make a note in your journal.

ONE LAST THING BEFORE YOU MOVE ON …

As we end this chapter, I'd like you to write a story about your search for knowledge, both looking back to your past and towards your future. It's not a big task; just take ten minutes to write without worry over grammar or spelling. I just want your immediate thoughts. You can always come back to it another time.

NOTES

1 Ainsworth, S., & Hardy, C. (2008). The enterprising self: An unsuitable job for an older worker. *Organization,* 15(3), 389–405.
2 Laceulle, H. (2018). Aging and the ethics of authenticity. *The Gerontologist,* 58(5), 970–978.
3 Atchley, R.C., & Robinson, J.L. (1982). Attitudes toward retirement and distance from the event. *Research on Aging,* 4, 299–313.
4 Tornstam, L. (2005). *Gerotranscendence: A Developmental Theory of Positive Aging.* Springer Publishing Company, New York.
5 Stephan, Y., Fouquereau, E., & Fernandez, A. (2008). The relation between self-determination and retirement satisfaction among active retired individuals. *The International Journal of Aging and Human Development,* 66(4), 329–345.

11

A CHANGE IN 'TIME'

Why you should read this chapter

This chapter covers the retirement transition, having a slower pace, and having additional time. The transition is a rite of passage and individuals can move into a different life, not as frantically paced and with more freedom and flexibility to do things on ones' own terms with a focus on new interests. With more control over ones' life, the pace can change, and people can focus on interests that satisfy them now. We are building on some of the areas covered earlier, and there are a number of activities to get you to reflect on specific areas. As we reach the end, I'll be asking you to write a story about these areas of your life, both looking back to your past and towards your future. There may be other details that resonate, so even if there isn't a specific activity feel free to pause and make a note in your journal and perhaps discuss with your buddy.

THE TRANSITION

Retirement is an important transition, a rite of passage like moving from school to university or to a first job. Without the structure of a job, people can feel unmoored and want to know how they fit into the world, what is their role. For some, like Sally, it is to be upfront: "I'm constantly thinking about where I want to be in this world." Constantly thinking implies it is at the forefront of her mind. Whilst she came to the interview as someone who said that she had found meaning, through our

DOI: 10.4324/9781003374206-14

conversation it appears that she is still searching, looking for her place.

Arthur spoke about how his work kept him grounded and anchored. He had left self-employment as it "didn't offer me any anchorage at all" and he wondered how he would get this without a job. In retirement he continues to travel but still needs stability, to 'be anchored', to feel grounded. This is who he is, and he spoke about this in earlier times. "I love experiencing new things, but I do like familiarity. I do like being anchored."

Some feel the pressure and urgency to find a role, albeit unpaid; they feel too young to do nothing and still feel a need to be productive and add value to the world. They are getting nervous, agitated, unsettled. Like Arthur, Sally is seeking to be anchored. She spoke about feeling unmoored and having to create structure. "I was really freaked out that I was going to feel unmoored." It seems that a lot of her identity, her reason for being, is tied up with being productive. She has a driver to be busy, and this can give her a sense of purpose. "I get a little nervous like. If I don't, well especially before the angel investing, if I didn't find something, how was I going to feel at 70 if I was unproductive between 57 and 70." She is looking forward and feels pressurised to act now; part of this transition to retirement could be to accept that this feeling of being unsettled is an important stage in her life development.

Activity 11.1

Where do you want to be in the world in the medium and longer term. Have you plans or even ideas for where you want to be five and ten years into the future? Make a note in your journal and you may like to discuss with your reflections buddy.

Some seek, like Sally, to create structure via a morning walk, classes, and voluntary work. Others can feel guilt. Sarah felt she had let down her colleagues and it took time to adjust to a differing pace. "I felt very guilty about not being there to do that job and help all the professors in the programme, I was their support staff; I took care of everything for them." Feeling guilt for leaving may hit Sarah more as much of her identity has been tied in with her job; she took care of her colleagues and had a nurturing approach to her work life.

"The transition period was very difficult, emotionally, because I had always been go, go, go". She needed time for the transition and to re-find who she was. Work that had been 'go, go, go,' was like a car screeching to a stop by slamming the breaks on; it is likely that a gentler phased retirement would have been helpful for her.

Arthur recognised the major life shift to a time of freedom without restrictions with both positive and negative aspects. Now he has no sense of dread about going into work. His work had been unhappy towards the end, and he was happy to leave. Now, after 45 years in a structured work environment, he relishes his freedom although found the lack of structure confusing, for example, at first losing track of the days.

> It does have the freedom, does have odd implications, you lose track of time, not only of days, but you also lose track of weeks, of months. And there's no sense of dread about going into work on a Monday. There's no sense of exhilaration about going into work on a Friday. There's no anticipation of weekends. Every day has got its own possibilities on a level basis. And that was one of the things that I've found not only very wonderful about retirement but also quite confusing.

He misses the anticipation of weekends, of having something to look forward to. Feeling exhilaration when going into work on Friday, implies excitement, and he has had to find his own excitement after retirement.

Activity 11.2

What will you miss in your daily routine when you no longer work? What will keep you moored and grounded as you lose the anchor of work? Make a note in your journal and you may like to discuss with your reflections buddy.

People who have used their intellectual intelligence at work don't want to step back completely. Claire stressed how she needed an intellectual aspect to retirement. For her this is nutritional therapy: "I can't not use my brain." Sally summed it up well, discussing how, now she is in charge of her day, she can do what she wants to do, not having to do things she would rather avoid. "Every day I think about what I want to do today. So, it's not like what I should do. It's like what I want to do." There is a newfound freedom, but it can take some adjusting to.

I wrote earlier how retirement is a major transition in older workers' lives and how up to a third of retirees find the transition stressful or see a decline in well-being. In my research, no one said it was stressful but there was a feeling of being unmoored (Sally), and a need to be anchored (Arthur). Some people will undertake bridge employment, but this can just delay the transition stage. What some of these people have done is to opt for encore careers, which is a pathway through which post-retirement individuals can (re)connect with their communities and continue to contribute in personally meaningful and socially worthwhile ways.

Activity 11.3

Look back at Chapter 4 where we considered alternatives to work. How are you feeling and what are your thoughts as you consider your alternatives? Have you clearly made a decision, or do you need to find out more? Make a note in your journal and you may like to discuss with your reflections buddy.

HAVING A SLOWER PACE

"I only want to work on the jewellery when I'm in the right headspace for it. In the morning, the space itself is very meditative, to me, open windows, looking out at the garden, I'm totally in another zone when I go in there. So, I love going in there." Many spoke about the busyness of the workplace and the adjustment needed to this next phase of life. For Sarah, it was to let things flow; she learned she didn't need to 'put her nose to the grindstone' and to choose to only work when she was in the right headspace. Too many people spend their time being full-on, without the time to 'smell the roses', so being able to work when she wants to is a welcome change for her. The move away from so much time focused on doing allows us to mature into elderhood with more time to focus and develop and share our wisdom.

This slower pace was appreciated by many – to be able to spend time with friends, to meet for coffee or a walk. To put, for example, home tasks on hold to be done another day and say yes to meeting a friend. COVID-19 made people like Helen realise that life is fragile, and you should say yes. "If my friend says, do you fancy coming to town? Instead of thinking to myself, actually, I'd planned to clean the wardrobes out or I planned to do the kitchen, it will be, yeah, I'll come. This has made me realise that life is fragile."

Meaning doesn't have to be about filling our days with doing; a meaningful life can include time with friends, time just to be, and also more time in the natural world. Helen recognises that her days had been 'full of work' and now she can appreciate that a life of meaning includes time just to be – something we can do once we step away from a busy full-time job. When our days are full of work, we can be on a treadmill, unable to come off, and no time to reflect on what is important to us. "It was wonderful, going into town and sitting and having a coffee and just looking at the world. It was something I had not done because I've been so full of work and all the other charitable stuff I'd done."

A slower pace can lead to a reduced focus on material possessions. Gerotranscendence[1] takes the focus away from acquisition and material success and helps to appreciate the world more for being as it is. This is a philosophy of leisure.[2] Now is the time when we should be happy with what we have rather than seeking something else. With Helen, it was to spend more time appreciating the simple things, such as time with a friend. Sarah chose to work on her jewellery when she wanted to, as part of a more balanced way of living. We often are proud to say how busy we are. A benefit of ageing and retirement is to be able to slow, stop, and reflect. We are told in life how we need to buy a new car, new phone, take more holidays ... but this all takes us away from being and experiencing life right now.

Activity 11.4

How do you think you will adjust to a slower pace? Who in your life will help and support your? It may take time to transition, so it is helpful to journal on this. And if you don't want to slow down you may want to reflect on why? Is it just not yet, or something deeper?

Nature

Everyone spoke of the need to spend time in nature, gardening, hiking, watching wildlife. They are finding meaning through spending time in nature; the fascination of watching the seasons change and focusing more deeply on the natural world. Arthur summed it up well: "Taking nature in, seeing how nature works round us, and with us, how nature, left to its own devices, would happily get on without us, the whole thing fascinates me."

Doug lives near a forest, and 200 yards from a major river; he spoke about his relationship with nature and specifically about how this is a way of having meaning in his life. "Multiple day outings in a kayak so I find meaning with nature. My relationship with nature and spirituality and the environment is a big part of my gratification for having moved out west." Being in a kayak, close to water, and feeling a part of the natural world; closeness to nature can make us feel alive and part of the greater universe which is giving a spiritual and natural connection to finding meaning.

Contact with nature is increasingly being recognised as contributing to humans' mental and physical health and has been linked to a reduction in mortality[3,4] and decreased risk of disease.[5] There is much research available with young people;[6] however, our interaction with nature does not end just because we age and as people move on to later stages of life more adults are seeking out a place to live with a greater connection to the natural environment.[7] Helen spent time in her garden, Doug kayaked to get close to nature, and Arthur was bird- and insect-watching. Empirical studies are increasingly documenting that immersion in nature predicts improvements in myriad health and well-being outcomes, and a meta-review of 59 papers found that contact with nature can reduce stress and promote a more robust health profile.[8]

Activity 11.5

You may like to reflect on your connection with nature. Is it in your garden, out in a wood, or in wild lands? Is it taking part in sports or using photography? Have you any ideas and plans for a greater connection? Take a moment to jot down your thoughts in your journal.

HAVING ADDITIONAL TIME

Retirement does not mean a total disengagement from work, rather it often means work on our own terms. Claire was able to step away from being on committees and focus on her well-being with a balance of healthy activities alongside using her gift for healing through Reiki and massage. "I just think you can't have regrets, in the long run. And that's what I want my retirement/ semi-retirement to be – the best life possible. And that's really, our philosophy on life. Now, more than ever, life's too short, you have to enjoy every moment."

Claire's comments resonated. I, too, don't want a life of regret. At this stage of life, looking back at decisions we have made and wishing they were different is not helpful. Now is a time to stop, and decide, where am I going in my life. For Claire it is to have the best life possible, stepping into her future with an openness and optimism; seeking less stress and finding a calling with the freedom to live her life the way that she wants to. She declares a philosophy of "life's too short, you have to enjoy every moment" and, indeed, at this stage in life we become more aware of our mortality. Enjoying every moment is saying yes to what you want to do and having the freedom to say no to those things that you don't want to do.

Activity 11.6

If you want your 'best life possible' what does this mean to you? I'm going to leave this as a broad question for you to write in your journal. Talk about this with your reflections buddy and also with any partner or other people close to you. How does your view match with theirs?

Retirement has allowed some to take on new interests, or to expand on a hobby. Sarah now had the time to pursue jewellery-making, and retirement was a time to restructure her life into how she wanted it to be and to escape the stress of a full-time job. The jewellery-making is clearly a calling for her. "Jewellery. Oh, that's a calling. Oh, totally, yes."

Helen had an interest in history throughout her life; now, in retirement, she could focus more on research, attending meetings and writing for publications. Like many, she has other interests too, around crafts and spending time in nature. Rose moved to Columbia and began with a focus on new friendships and interests, helping her to understand more about who she is. She is meeting people like herself, who are focusing on their personal growth.

Here I am living in a foreign country trying to learn the language to survive, and all of a sudden, I'm surrounded by all these women who are like-minded, who are interested in doing internal work and focusing on their personal growth. And it was such a beautiful opportunity to develop meaningful lasting intimate relationships with women.

Rose is having a meaningful life in Columbia; here she found her purpose mentoring young women through the creation of a social enterprise. She is connecting with them, and caring for their development, taking on a mentoring role, and feeling relevant. This is allowing her to give back and to have formed long-lasting relationships.

Is finding their place in the world harder for people like Doug and Arthur who had a calling in their work? Both gained a great deal of satisfaction from their occupation. "It was the fourth job, the one that I thought I couldn't do that really liberated me. And that that was quite an extraordinary feeling. When I moved to my final place of work there was a different element to work." For Arthur, it was a change of management style that led him to take retirement. He had spoken earlier about huge enthusiasm; here he is using the word extraordinary. These epic descriptions capture how he can feel with work that gets him into the zone. He now has a new-found passion and huge enthusiasm for watching live music, through gig writing and photography.

For Doug, whose leadership consulting was 'helping people to grow into their future best self', it was after a second marriage and moving across country that he decided to stop looking for work and see what happens, maintaining some very part-time work in this area and alongside time in nature, with a new interest setting up a series of music concerts in his village, choosing who to invite and seeing the music promotion as "the real crux of my meaning-making in my ageing period."

Activity 11.7

Where do you want to focus your time? What is going to give meaning to your life? It doesn't have to be 'mega'; it can be made up of smaller moments. Make a note of any ideas in your journal.

Having additional time allows people time to take on more activity and to develop and expand on relationships with others. Social relationships are important for the retirement adjustment[9,10] but are rarely considered as people plan for retirement. Much research will talk about the benefits of marriage to a better retirement adjustment,[11] but others have found no support for this,[12] which may well be down to the quality of the relationship; not every marriage is a happy one. Only high-quality marital relationships enhance life satisfaction in retirement.[13]

Our well-being can be kept strong through wider relationships with friends.[14] Social groups can help, meeting up with friends, being part of a class, such as Sally's art group and Helen's history groups, and family and friendship groups. These groups are part of our social identity[15] and are part of understanding who we are, our self-definition, such as members of the Watson family, members of the historical society, people who watch live music at independent venues. They can also provide support and connection.[16]

It is because of our connection with groups that we can experience feelings of loss on retirement. Evidence shows that in retirement, social contact is the biggest loss, although this concern is less common, the longer people are retired.[17] To have new social groups lined up for when we leave the workplace will enhance our transition. The more groups a person belongs to, the more likely it is that he or she will have access to resources that support and promote adjustment to life change.[18]

Activity 11.8

We spoke about relationships in Chapter 8. What groups are you connected to, and, if still working, have you plans to join groups beyond your workplace? Make a note in your journal.

ONE LAST THING BEFORE YOU MOVE ON …

As we end this chapter. I'd like you to write a story about these areas of your life, both looking back to your past and towards your future. It's not a big task; just take ten minutes to write without worry over grammar or spelling. I just want your immediate thoughts. You can always come back to it another time.

NOTES

1 Tornstam, L. (2005). *Gerotranscendence: A Developmental Theory of Positive Aging*. Springer Publishing Company, New York.

2 Pieper J. (1963). *Leisure: The Basis of Culture*. Ignatius Press, San Francisco.

3 James, P., Hart, J.E., Banay, R.F., & Laden, F. (2016). Exposure to greenness and mortality in a nationwide prospective cohort study of women. *Environmental Health Perspectives*, 124, 1344–1352.

4 Richardson, E., Pearce, J., Mitchell, R., Day, P., & Kingham, S. (2010). The association between green space and cause-specific mortality in urban New Zealand: An ecological analysis of green space utility. *BMC Public Health*, 10, 240.

5 Maas, J., Verheij, R.A., de Vries, S., Spreeuwenberg, P., Schellevis, F.G., & Groenewegen, P.P. (2009). Morbidity is related to a green living environment. *Journal of Epidemiology and Community Health*.

6 Rantala, O., & Puhakka, R., (2019). Engaging with nature: Nature affords well-being for families and young people in Finland. *Children's Geographies*.

7 Carman, J. (2011). Elders' lifelong connection with the natural environment. *Educational Gerontology*, 37(6), 488–498.

8 Hartig, T., Mitchell, R., de Vries, S., & Frumkin, H. (2014). Nature and health. *Annual Review of Public Health*, 35, 207–228.

9 Taylor-Carter, M.A., Cook, K., & Weinberg, C. (1997). Planning and expectations of the retirement experience. *Educational Gerontology*, 23, 273–288.

10 Yeung, D.Y., & Zhou, X., (2017). Planning for retirement: Longitudinal effect on retirement resources and post-retirement well-being. *Frontiers in Psychology*, 8, 1–14.

11 Etaugh, C., & Bridges, J. (2013). *Women's Lives: A Psychological Perspective* (3rd ed.). Allyn and Bacon, Boston, MA.

12 Pinquart, M., & Schindler, I. (2007). Changes of life satisfaction in the transition to retirement: A latent-class approach. *Psychology and Aging*, 22(3), 442–455.

13 Kim, J.E., & Moen, P. (2001). Moving into retirement: Preparation and transitions in late midlife. In M.E. Lachman (Ed.), *Handbook of Midlife Development* (487–527). John Wiley, New York.

14 Damman, M., & van Duijn, R. (2017). Intergenerational support in the transition from work to retirement. *Work Aging and Retirement*, 3, 66–76.

15 Tajfel, H. & Turner, J.C. (1979). An integrative theory of intergroup conflict. In W.G. Austin & S. Worchel (Eds.), *The Social Psychology of Intergroup Relations* (33–47). Brooks-Cole, Monterey, CA.
16 Cruwys, T., Haslam, S.A., Dingle, G.A., Haslam, C., & Jetten, J. (2014b). Depression and social identity: An integrative review. *Personality and Social Psychology Review*, 18, 215–238.
17 Damman, M., Hènkens, K., & Kalmijn, M. (2015). Missing work after retirement: The role of life histories in the retirement adjustment process. *The Gerontologist*, 55(5), 802–813.
18 Jetten, J., Haslam, C., Haslam, S. A., Dingle, G., & Jones, J. M. (2014). How groups affect our health and well-being: the path from theory to policy. *Social Issues and Policy Review*, 8, 103–130.

12

WHO AM I?

Why you should read this chapter

In this chapter you again get to read and learn from the stories of the people I interviewed. It covers the important theme of identity and the question of 'Who am I?' We start with the search for a new identity, then move onto family background – have we achieved things because of family support or despite the family relationship? We also look at bravery, rebellion, and the value of being of service. Our self-understanding can lead to inner strength, and will allow us to recognise both our intelligence and capability. Knowing who you are, what is important, the need to create a purpose can all help with finding meaning in life. You are introduced to possible selves. These are future conceptions of the self and provide possibilities of who we could be in the future.

Carl Jung said: "Looking outwards has got to be turned into looking into oneself. Discovering yourself provides you with all you are, were meant to be, and all you are living from and for." Growing older can mean we can look back, take account of the journey to where we are now, and review the future of our life.

THE SEARCH FOR A NEW IDENTITY

The retiree identity has a psychological reality for people undergoing the retirement transition and this can be a helpful resource in this time of significant life change.[1] To what

DOI: 10.4324/9781003374206-15

extent do people like us want to identify with a group known as 'retired'? Social identity is seen to be particularly influential in the lead-up to retirement, when we engage with the possibility that we will give up work. Having a positive image of retirees in the lead-up to retirement provided a basis for the motivation both to retire and to connect with other retirees.[2]

For many, their identity is closely related to their employment, so retirement brings a loss of identity and the need to find a new one. In retirement, we need to let go of an older identity, for example, for Helen, identity as a barrister, and to move to a new one; Helen now defines herself as a local historian. This can be a positive if we did not enjoy our work, but for people who are highly invested in their work it is seen as a loss.[3]

It is only after retirement that many people, especially men, realise how much of their identity was connected to their work.[4] One way to avoid this is to continue to work. People who continue with bridge employment and extensive voluntary work may be doing this to strengthen their continuity with their work identity, despite having formally retired.

Through the transition to retirement, we can become clearer on the person we have become, what our identity is now, rather than saying that we are, for example, a retired teacher or former barrister. Helen has focused on historical research, writing, and studies; this has giving her a new identity as an historian. She wants to be defined in the way that fits her now. She has made a clear break; being a barrister is the end of the old story. "And if it comes up in conversation that I was a barrister, end of story, but it doesn't define who I am. I'd rather be known as the local historian, to be frank."

As part of Arthur's expanding interest in photography, he combined this with his love of writing, developed during his career to undertake reviewing for music magazines. He talked about the impact he has had; people see him as an influencer in this area. This can be seen as a fantastic achievement, and he is clearly influential.

> I know for a fact that one artist pulled a 30-date UK tour as an opening act for an A-list headliner on the strength of two reviews. I've also assisted with university entrance

applications to study music and grant applications to further music careers. The satisfaction I get when I hear that an application has been successful is considerable.

Activity 12.1

How do you describe yourself when people ask, 'And what do you do?' Are you happy to say you are retired, or semi-retired. Do you refer to your previous identity. Make a note and also consider if this is the right one for you; you can change it at any time.

Self-awareness

Before getting a new identity, we need to know who we are through self-awareness. Self-awareness is something that generally grows with age; we learn more about ourselves and have more confidence. Doug said: "The whole dimension of the inner spiritual growth and the opportunity to be a lifelong learner and believe that there's always self-development and introspection, is a valuable aspect of the path that I'm on." As a life-long learner he understands himself more through introspection. He is on a path, sees his life as a journey, and will continue to grow through further looking within.

> When I was younger, I believed in the term 'fake it till you make it' and I spent a lot of years feeling like I was faking it. I didn't know that I was a strong person. When my second husband had the head injury, I had to find my strengths, and I realised that I was very strong and very powerful and very intelligent, very capable. I never knew those things.

For some people, like Sarah, it is to pretend; to 'fake it till you make it' but then something happens, and you get some inner strength and realise that you are capable. Sarah came to a greater self-understanding and as she learned more about herself, it was no longer necessary to pretend. With Sarah's husband badly injured, she dealt with the situation, and, like Helen, found her inner strength. She found out that she was 'a strong person'. She felt powerful, her identity was changing, she realised that she was capable. No longer held back, she had inner confidence. It is very powerful to realise that you do have strengths, to recognise your intelligence, and that you are capable; to take this and move forward in life.

Self-awareness was important to Rose.

> I believe, that in order to find meaning you have to find yourself first, your core self, like when nobody's looking. Who am I, and what matters to me, and I could not have been committed to this project when I first arrived in Colombia four years ago, because I had not aligned myself with myself. I truly believe that that's the first step in finding meaning. Well, the first step is recognising that I'm not feeling meaning. And then the second step is what does that mean to me. And who's me.

She wanted to understand her core self, the authentic person within, rather than how she has appeared to the world in the past. She spoke about alignment, and earlier had spoken about being out of alignment in many aspects of her life. Knowing who you are, what is important, the need to create a purpose can all help with finding meaning in life.

Rose had taken a step, as Carl Jung has described, to ask, 'Who am I?' and to ascertain what matters to her. Important steps before starting a new life in Columbia. These are deep questions at any stage of life, but particularly as we move into the 20 or so years of life after full-time working. Understanding who we are, thinking about what matters, what gives us meaning, is a very powerful stage to reach.

As we answer the question 'Who am I?', we are in the development goal of finding our authentic self. There are different definitions of the authentic, or 'true self'. Maslow,[5] includes self-actualisation; for Harter,[6] authenticity involves owning one's personal thoughts, emotions, desires, preferences, or beliefs. Horney[7] discusses the consequences of constructing a false self, resulting in individuals feeling alienated from their true selves.

Activity 12.2

Let's take the broad question 'Who am I?' and make notes in our journal. It may be free-flowing writing, it might be a series of bullet points. The important thing is to get things out of your head and onto paper so you can review them. Then take a step back; do you like what you wrote? Are there any areas you want to change? For some people, it is to change a personality factor, such as to be more assertive or less bossy.

Erikson's[8] model of personality development can lead to struggles with identity, as experienced at different life stages such as identity versus role confusion (the adolescence and young adulthood stage). Now at the generativity vs. stagnation virtue of care, this can be the time to review our life to date, although most people will not consciously use a psychological model. This can be nostalgic, as we remember the past or have regret for lost opportunities.[9] We also have the loss of relationships, challenges, and activities and there is a need to allow space for consideration of what to do at this stage of life, now with a recognition of the finite nature of life, and to allow alternative identities to emerge.[10] To become more of the person we want to be.

Activity 12.3

You may like to look back on your life and think of loss and regrets. We can grieve for poor decisions and lost relationships and to see what we have learned from them. You may like to reflect on this and write things down in your journal. As I write this, I've learned about the recent death of a friend and wish I'd met up with him in the past couple of months. I will make a more conscious effort to stay in touch with friends.

Still searching

Not everyone has found their place in the world. People can feel that they have found meaning in life but, as we explored things, it became clearer that whilst Sally is busy, when she says "Maybe I'll find something that will really drive me", it leads to a view that she could be looking for something deeper. "The blog is kind of keeping my mind active, it's only once a month … kind of is giving back, it's focused on lessons from my career and my life." She is looking for a way to give back, via her blog which she says is "kind of giving back", so she recognises this is not enough and there is a need for something deeper.

At age 58, she was one of the younger participants and our conversation covered the pressure that she feels under to make use of her potential and not to just coast through the life ahead of her, recognising that much of her mental energy is spent on this. Is she looking for too much, setting impossible to reach standards? Possibly, when she says that she is looking for an organisation – "like it might, that it melts my heart." Her current range of interests and activities seem to be filling the void that could be filled if she found the one passionate pursuit.

Claire is exploring if she had wasted her talent.

> It's been a driver for me all my life. It's the question that scares me. Because if I think too deeply about it, I think, have I wasted my talent, because I am not prime minister, I am not Bill Gates, I am not that massive person. And I believe I could have been any of those things, that self-belief that my dad gave me. I absolutely believe I could have done any of that stuff. I wasn't the ground-breaking heart surgeon, whatever. So, when I think about legacy, I have to stop trying to be perfect.

Fiercely intelligent, and with a father who gave her the self-belief that she could be anything she wanted, she is now feeling that she could have achieved more, that this is the time to do something 'mega'. But does it have to be?

She is making an impact into the lives of all the people who come to her for therapy. That could be seen as enough and a better way of viewing life – embracing what she has done rather than being wistful for what was missed. 'Have I wasted my talent?' is a deep question to reflect on; I could have been any of those things. Yes, we all face 'sliding door moments' when we can make choices, but what we can lose is supplemented by what we can also gain. Earlier she had spoken about not having regrets, but although she said this, there is still a part of her that can wonder about what may have been. As we search for meaning, we are at a point where we look back, and sometimes it is with regrets; this is part of the process of moving ahead. Claire says that she will stop trying to be perfect, and this means accepting ourselves as human.

Possible selves

When people are still searching, it may be that they need to consider their 'possible selves'.[11] Possible selves are future conceptions of the self and provide possibilities of who we could be in the future, and also what we are concerned we may become.[12] These concerns could include being old and insignificant, and perhaps no longer mattering, which we covered in Chapter 9. Being aware of possible selves can motivate us to move towards a goal. Whilst possible selves can be considered across the life span, from middle age the possible selves are more realistic,[13] and an increase in life satisfaction in older adults may be due to a more realistic view of aspirations to when people were younger.[14]

Activity 12.4

1. You may like to reflect on past possible selves, on what you could have been. Don't spend too long on this, but it is useful to get how we could have been down on paper so we can accept the decisions we made.
2. Think to the future and imagine everything goes well. Spend about ten minutes writing on this in your journal without over-thinking it.

FAMILY BACKGROUND

Our family can have a major impact on who we are; it can influence us, both in a positive and negative way. Someone can take hardship as a reason not to succeed, whilst for another person it drives them forward. We also get messages that we absorb into how to be with others. Some people have highly supportive parents, giving them the confidence to do anything. Whilst this can be seen as inspiring, Claire was also left with a 'Be perfect' driver, which has both driven her and had a negative impact. This has led to Claire, who was academically able and could be seen as successful, questioning whether she could have done more with her life.

> My dad absolutely believed we could do anything in the world. He was very passionate about our capabilities, and particularly mine, so I, ended up as a 'Be perfect' child. And that has been quite a significant driver for a long time, both in a positive and a negative sense, but I've also had a very strong sense of I can do anything.

For Helen, who was brought up by grandparents, and without the support of her mother, family gave her a drive to do well; was this a way that she was seeking praise from an absent parent? It may well have led to her stoicism and to deal well with hardships and setbacks.

> My grandfather ran the District Scout Group … my father was a District Commissioner of Scouts and right from an early age, my grandmother told me that I was very lucky to have what I got, and I've got to give something back to the community. So, all my life, that has been at the back of my mind. I've always done voluntary work. I ran a Brownie pack in my village when I was 16, which was far too young, but I got a letter from Mabel Baden Powell to tell me I could run it. So, I got my warrant to run it.

She was told by her grandparents that she was lucky and speaks about the importance to 'give back', which led to voluntary work, including getting special dispensation to run a Brownie pack at age 16. The message of service was one she followed in life. "I've got to give something back to the community" is a strong driver for service and a value she has followed.

For Rose, estranged from family, she ran away at 16 and focused on getting a job that paid very well and later, perhaps for survival, sought the security of marriage. "I had been estranged from my family, from my parents, for decades and decades. I grew up in New York, and I ran away to California, at age 16. So, essentially my life was about survival." When she says that her life was about survival, that's not looking for meaning in life but for the very basic needs that must be met like food and shelter. Part of her way of dealing with this unhappy childhood is to help others who have inner challenges to deal with. She now has a clear purpose in life with the young women she works with, offering a supportive environment for them.

Activity 12.5

Look back at your childhood and consider the messages you gained from your parents; how have these made you the person you are to-day? Have they had a positive influence or is everything you achieved despite your childhood? Is there still any impact on you now, from parents or siblings, or do the messages resonate around your head? Take some time to think about this and write it down.

BRAVERY AND REBELLION

Many of the participants were seen as rebels in their younger days. I was a bit of a hippy as a teenager and when Arthur spoke of his difficulty getting a job because of his long hair, it resonated, as my male friends had the same problem. "I had some difficulty finding a job in the first place because my hair was very, very long, way down past my shoulders."

Several had not wanted to be seen as the same as other people and explored life through the work of Carlos Castaneda,

Herman Hesse, and *Zen and the Art of Motorcycle Maintenance* – books that I also had read. Sarah had dropped out to travel across America on a motorbike with her boyfriend and moved to Hawaii. "I had a grand adventure. My boyfriend and I got married, shortly after high school … we bought a motorcycle, we bought backpacks and tents and a couple changes of clothes."

Claire was pushing boundaries and being rebellious in her teen years and could be seen as a radical feminist; Helen was a rebel in a different way, studying to be an electrician, quite unusual back in the 1970s. Claire said "I loved school, I loved being there, but I had a very tense relationship with my dad. Because I was pushing every boundary and trying to be rebellious. I was a quite rebellious teenager, from his perspective." For Doug, it was to spend time in a retreat community that could be seen as 'dropping out' even if it wasn't long term. "I got to do the retreat at the ashram in Australia, … that was a highlight of my international travel and opportunities that came from networking.". Over 50 per cent of the participants were willing to take a step out of the norm, and I see this as them seeking to be more authentic, being true to who they are rather than to fit in.

Authenticity in marriage

Whilst divorce was becoming more common in the 1980s it takes courage to decide to leave a marriage and travel, and to leave not because you have found someone new, or indeed for cruelty, but because "I can't become who I'm supposed to be if I stay in the confines of this marriage." There is a need to find the authentic you, the path chosen by Rose.

Rose said:

> My husband forced the question of whether I was going to stay in the marriage or not. … What it came down to, after a brutal soul-searching, was that I can't become who I'm supposed to be if I stay in the confines of this marriage.

She spoke of the need to find her core self, saying that this would be impossible if remaining married. I take this to mean a search for authenticity, about being true to who she is rather than to portray herself in a particular way; it takes courage to show up as our true self. For Rose, this internal search came as she explored freedom at the end of her marriage, recognising that you can be trapped in a marriage.

Activity 12.6

You may like to spend time to reminisce on the happy times of your teens and young adulthood, when you were carefree. Also, to consider your relationships; to what extent can you be truly yourself? Ours is an age when we can focus on the importance of being who we are, and we need a relationship that supports this. This is something worth journalling about.

THE VALUE OF BEING OF SERVICE

Underpinning many of the interviews was a need to be of service, and for several, this was also important before retirement. Doug talked about being of service to others through his work, and the positive impact he has made with contacts from across the world. "Everything that I've done has been about helping people learn and grow and be of service in their settings that they live and work in. So those are among my core values." Understanding our core values is helpful in finding meaning, as we are clearer on what is important to us. Doug said that everything that he had done had been about helping people learn and grow, and this was an important part of his identity. He spoke about being of service as being a core value.

Helen talked about her values of service and responsibility that showed itself in various aspects of her earlier life, and now through community work. "I ran the Civic Society on top of working as well. It was instilled in me as a child to give something back." Earlier I discussed her work running Guide and Brownie packs, but there was more. Being of service was core to her being; it was instilled in her from childhood that she needed to give back, and this has given her a sense of purpose throughout her life.

For Sally, working for the government, she saw her job as being for the people, and now, in retirement, sought to be of service further through voluntary work. She created a blog to give back, as a way of continuing the mentoring of younger people which she did whilst working. "The blog is helpful because at least I feel like I'm giving back to something – that is contributing." She uses the word 'feel' and that's important; but is feeling enough for her? The tone to her voice was more tentative; she is seeking more. She is seeking to know, and will find this as she gains deeper meaning in her life.

Being of service can relate to mattering, which is an individual's perception that they make a difference in the world. We spoke about mattering in Chapter 9 and how mattering provides a sense of social meaning (one's meaning to others) and relatedness (the degree to which one matters to the world). A lack of feelings of mattering can mean a person feels invisible, and not recognised and peripheral to their social context.[15]

Retirement can be when some people step up to the role of elder, and this can involve support to younger people as pursued by Rose and Sally. Rose said: "I mentioned the friend asking me for mentoring on the financial plan. I've since then helped a handful of young women, in planning how they can be living my lifestyle when they're my age", and Sally said: "That was something I did a lot of in my job. The young people came to me and I did a lot of speaking to younger professionals". Being of service is a way for people to be able to share their wisdom with the wider world. Rose has helped a handful of young women, but her impact has helped many, running personal development sessions for groups of women. Sally used to talk with younger professionals at work and was now able to utilise the knowledge that she had gained whilst employed within her blog.

Activity 12.7

To what extent do you want to be of service? Have you any plans to mentor or to give back? Make a note of any thoughts you have on this below; then why not schedule a time to talk with your reflections buddy?

There is often a tension between work and leisure and where the retiree should focus time and energy. There is a dichotomy around wanting to be productive and work and a focus on leisure.[16] The tension can be modified by a greater focus on generativity during retirement (which we covered in Chapter 9) and through mentoring activity in the community.[17]

Values

Our new identify can include greater clarity on our values. For Claire, these haven't changed, and she clearly listed them: "I don't think my values have changed that much if I'm honest. I think my values have always been around authenticity. I think they've always been around feeling productive, making a difference, integrity, and fairness." Life may well be simpler when through your life you can live to your values; with Claire this included authenticity, integrity, and fairness.

Integrity was important to Sarah too, alongside trust and honesty. She spoke about the importance of being herself within a relationship, and of acceptance.

> Trust is huge. Integrity is huge, being truthful, sincere, honest. All of those things are very big to me. Family is important. Relationships, you know. I think being transparent in relationships. Like just being able to completely be yourself and trusting that the person you're in relationship with is totally okay with whoever, they just accept you.

Being accepted, "being able to completely be yourself", not having to pretend or put on a fake front – we have previously read about Helen's desire to be of service, and this stems from her values: "I definitely believe in giving something back to society. That's something that came with me from when I was a child, and I hate to see selfishness in people who could give and don't."

Sometimes values are hidden in earlier life, as we try to fit in; but now is the time for them to come to the fore. This was covered well by Rose:

I think, if I'm being truly honest, I would say that they have always been my values, the values of service, of giving back, and abundance. I think that really plays into everything I do and believe. There were years in my life that those values were not on the surface, that there were other values that I was living by, that were taking a higher priority. And that's very likely what led to the feeling of misalignment.

She said she has always had values of service and giving back, but in the past they were below the surface, other things took priority. She was able to follow these values while living in Columbia, supporting local people with their business ideas and social impact. We can be driven by values that seem more important to us when we are younger – the values that society deem important, about striving to be a success at work, having status, and financial rewards. It is only as we age that many of us realise that these things are not important. Doug has been helping people learn and grow and to be of service to others throughout his life and continues to do so.

I would say that at the core of my values was personal growth and adult and lifelong learning. So, everything that I've done has been about helping people learn and grow and be of service in their settings that they live in work in. So those are among my core values.

Activity 12.8

You identified your values back in Chapter 4. You may like to review them again and consider how they have changed over your life and the extent you currently live a life in line with your values. You can journal your thoughts and perhaps discuss with your reflections buddy.

BEFORE YOU MOVE ON ...

You have been thinking deeply at a number of areas in this chapter. You may like to now review them and consider how these events have made you who you are. Is being of service important to you now? If you were a rebel when younger, are there ways you could use the same qualities now? What was the impact of your family background? As we end this chapter, you may like to write a story about how the stories in this chapter have impacted on 'Who am I now?' and any reflections from the past or thoughts for the future before we move on to the final chapter. You may also like to talk with your reflections buddy about this.

NOTES

1 Michinov, E., Fouquereau, E., & Fernandez, A. (2008). Retirees' social identity and satisfaction with retirement. *The International Journal of Aging and Human Development*, 66(3), 175–194.

2 Gaillard, M., & Desmette, D. (2008). Intergroup predictors of older workers' attitudes towards work and early exit. *European Journal of Work and Organizational Psychology*, 17(4), 450–481.

3 Wang, M. (2007). Profiling retirees in the retirement transition and adjustment process: Examining the longitudinal change patterns of retirees' psychological well-being. *Journal of Applied Psychology*, 92, 455–474.

4 Szinovacz, M.E., & De Viney, S. (1999). The retiree identity: Gender and race differences. *Journals of Gerontology: Series B: Psychological Sciences & Social Sciences*, 54B, S207–S218.

5 Maslow, A.H. (1968). *Toward a Psychology of Being* (2nd ed.). Van Nostrand, New York.

6 Harter, S. (2002). Authenticity. In Snyder, C.R., & Lopez, S.J. (Eds.), *Handbook of Positive Psychology* (382–394). Oxford University Press, New York.

7 Horney, K. (1950). *Neurosis and Human Growth: The Struggle Toward Self-Realization*. W. W. Norton, Oxford.

8 Erikson, E. H. (1963). *Childhood and Society* (2nd ed.). Norton, New York.

9 Osborne, J.W. (2012). Psychological effects of the transition to retirement. *Canadian Journal of Counselling and Psychotherapy*, 46(1), 45–58.

10 Gilleard, C., & Higgs, P. (2007). The third age and the baby boomers: Two approaches to the social structuring of later life. *International Journal of Ageing and Later Life*, 2(2), 13–30.

11 Kloep, M., & Hendry, L. B. (2006). Pathways into retirement: Entry or exit? *Journal of Occupational and Organizational Psychology*, 79, 569–593.

12 Markus, H., & Paula N. (1986). Possible selves. *American Psychologist*, 41(9), 954–969.

13 Cross, S., & Markus, H. (1991). Possible selves across the life span. *Human Development*, 34(4), 230–255.

14 Campbell, A., Converse, P.E., & Rodgers, W.L. (1976). *The Quality of American Life*. Sage, New York.

15 Schultheiss, O.C., & Pang, J.S. (2007). Measuring implicit motives. In R.W. Robins, R.C. Fraley, & R.F. Krueger (Eds.), *Handbook of Research Methods in Personality Psychology* (322–344). The Guilford Press.

16 James, J.B., Morrow-Howell, N., Gonzales, E., Matz-Costa, C., & Riddle-Wilder, A. (2020) Beyond the livelong workday: Is there a new face of retirement? In: Czaja, S., Sharit, J., & James, J. (Eds.), *Current and Emerging Trends in Aging and Work*. Springer, Cham

17 Miranda-Chan, T., & Nakamura, J. (2016). A generativity track to life meaning in retirement: Ego-integrity returns on past academic mentoring investments. *Work, Aging and Retirement*, 2, 24–37.

Mitchell, R., & Popham, F. (2008). Effect of exposure to natural environment on health inequalities: An observational population study. *Lancet*, 372, 1655–1660.

13

THE NEW YOU

Why you should read this chapter

This final chapter is a time to review our journey, to reflect on how much we have learned and how far we have come. The book is aimed at the young-olds, the early part of later life where many remain in good health. You will again be asked to write on what is a successful retirement to you and we will return to important areas such as health and relationships. You will consider your best possible self, to provide you with a blueprint to work towards. The chapter also considers how our life is a story, having an authentic life, elderhood and legacy. We end with imagining being 90 and looking back at our life.

And now we come to the final chapter. A time to review our journey, to reflect on how much we have learned and how far we have come. From an understanding of transitions, and finding out where we are now, we have looked deep within, considered work, what it means to us, and work alternatives, alongside a review of our health and well-being, our relationships, and taking stock on financial areas. We then took a deeper dive into meaning and learned more about how mattering and generativity help us in this stage of life.

Back in the first chapter, I spoke about the y-olds, and that's who we are. The young-olds. Many of us will remain in good health and be leading active lives. This period takes us to about the age of 75 when, using researcher definitions, we move into the 'old' category, with 'old-old' coming later. So, my focus in

DOI: 10.4324/9781003374206-16

this book is the part of retirement where we generally remain in good health and are getting things in place for later life. I appreciate that some readers may have health challenges, and may need to dig into their internal optimist, and look for how to adapt to the situation they are in; no one knows when we will reach this point.

Our age is a time for greater meaning in life; to work towards a legacy and to give back. My wider interest lies in how people can move beyond being seen as old to being a respected elder within society, able to share wisdom and contribute from a position in life that people will want to aspire to and that is the focus for my next book. In Western society we don't have a tradition of older people moving up to the role of elder which provides people with a purpose and meaning; this is more common in Indigenous societies. However, being an elder is about much more than age: it is about knowing oneself and having a focus wider than the self.[1,2] We now have the freedom to reconsider what is important to us and focus on personal development.[3]

Meaning relates to our life mattering, that our life has meaning. This can be with the wider world or with our community, that we will be remembered when we are gone. Meaning in life has been correlated with psychological adjustment, hope, and vitality;[4] these are particularly pertinent for well-being at a time of change, such as retirement.

I believe it is important to continue to find ways to serve the world, considering we now live on average 30 to 40 years longer than a century ago. These extra years can be utilised to make a positive impact. Instead of viewing ageing as a negative, we can see it as time to make a difference with others and the wider world. Leading a life of purposeful engagement not only keeps us happy but also healthier.

In Chapter 5 we considered how we can use the time we have left. It may be to continue to work but to have a more flexible approach and also to ensure that what we do has meaning. Whilst a certain level of income may be needed, to what extent does our activity nurture our soul? We can also look again at our relationships. Do we need to reach out and make our peace with others and to deal with any regrets, for example?

WHAT SORT OF RETIREMENT DO YOU WANT?

At the end of the first chapter, I asked you to write a letter to yourself on: What does a successful retirement look like to you?

Activity 13.1

You may like to read it again and to see whether there is anything to add. Did you include anything on how you would find meaning, on your relationships, any changes to become healthier? You can now revise it if your views have changed or you can add to it.

I don't want you to plan for the long term, but to focus on the next two years and then the next five. We can review further ahead later. For now, it is about gaining some clarity, providing a blueprint of your life to give you focus.

Activity 13.2

I'd like you to reflect on these key areas that we covered in Chapter 3. Reflect on the areas that follow and make a note of your answers in your journal.

Health

What are your current thoughts on what to do for now, and then two and five years into the future? Do you need to make changes to how you eat, how much you drink, levels of activity, to exercise more or differently, maybe to look for ways to relieve stress and increase well-being?

Relationships

Retirement will lead to changes in your relationship with your partner or spouse, and so there is a need to share goals with them. You may want to share your views on life ahead: will you start new interests together or maintain some independence? Do you need to give more help to your elderly parents or other older relatives? If you have siblings, is this something to discuss as a family? We only have so much time and energy, so it may be worth finding out what external help is available.

You may also like to consider wider relationships with friends and your wider social network It's in our 60s that we often realise we focused on work to the detriment of maintaining friendships. We can make new connections via hobbies and interests such as volunteering and joining groups. I joined a comedy improv group and several meet-up groups related to my interests, making friends through all of them. We can also get in touch with old friends and may be able to rekindle friendships. Having friendships across generations is important too.

Employment, interests, and personal growth

What are your current thoughts on what to do for now, and then two and five years ahead? Should you continue with your current employer or a similar role for the foreseeable future? Move to something you have always loved to do, even if it means a significant pay cut? Move to a less stressful, but, hopefully, still fulfilling job? Perhaps part-time work to allow more time for other interests or to stop any paid work? Should you take up a new hobby or allow more time for a current interest? Take a course, either academic studies or non-vocational, such as genealogy or photography; focus on voluntary work or is it more informal development through reading and joining groups?

Activity 13.3

Considering our (best possible) future self comes from positive psychology and is known to enhance well-being.[5] It involves thinking about yourself in the future. For example, imagine your family life and write down everything that is going well, thinking of your partner, children, parents, and siblings. It is the best you can imagine. You created a version of this in Chapter 3 so you may like to review your notes from then. Write for ten minutes, being as detailed as you wish. You can do the same with other aspects of your life, such as your work, your health, and your relationships and also your social life and your leisure activities.

At our stage of life, I recommend we look at these areas separately, but we also take a broader view of our retirement – how will it be if it is as good as it can be?

Activity 13.4

We are moving on from the last activity. That was looking at things individually and there may be a great deal of realism to what you wrote. In this activity, the focus is on your best possible self when life is as good as it ever could be.

Imagine it is two (or five) years from now; what will your retirement be like? Think of the best possible option where everything goes well. Think about what you will be doing – work or something else; consider your health, your relationships, your spiritual connection. Spend 10 to 15 minutes writing it down and making it as detailed as possible. I gave an example of my future self, back in chapter 3. You may like to then discuss this with your reflections buddy.

YOUR LIFE AS A STORY

You are fascinating. Whatever your background, you have an interesting story to tell. No one has ever lived your life with your successes and challenges, failures and dreams. As we look back on our life and what we remember, some of it is factual and known to be true, but other aspects are based on our interpretation of events; we can see something challenging and maybe disappointing as a chance to learn and grow or we could remain focused on the negative. As you look back, it is this reflection of our life that informs our current experience, providing growth and understanding.[6] We understand through stories, as found in many books and many films such as the *Star Wars* and *Harry Potter* franchises.

The hero's journey

The hero's journey is a common pattern that many great adventure stories follow. This journey typically includes three critical phases. The first stage is *the call to adventure*, which spurs the potential hero into taking courageous action, often involving a daunting task such as battling Goliath or defeating the Empire. The second stage is *the ordeal*, a gruelling test that challenges the hero's abilities and perseverance, such as taking a giant on in combat or obliterating the Death Star. The third stage is *the victory*, where the hero overcomes insurmountable obstacles and emerges triumphant, returning home a success.

According to psychoanalyst Carl Jung, successful people tend to view their lives through the framework of this mythical journey. It is through facing these challenges that we get a deeper understanding of our abilities, limitations, and the person we are. This is how we have lived our lives; we have gone through the 'battle' to reach the pinnacle of our career. But then it ends.

The story never talked about is what it is like when the hero returns home to a mundane life where no one is interested in how you saved the world, and you still need to take the bins out and do the washing. Life is different when you no longer have the power. I'm reminded of a quote by Retired US General Norman Schwarzkopf: "Seven months ago I could give a single command and 541,000 people would immediately obey it. Today, I can't get a plumber to come to my house." It is this change that leads to the feeling of being unmoored; the obvious answer for many is to carry on working, but it still needs addressing sometime.

This final stage to the hero's journey is what Joseph Campbell[7] calls 'the crossing of the return threshold'. This is the return to real life with different challenges ahead. In this final stage – retirement – eventually our successes will cease to shine brightly, our skills will decline, and too, in time, will our health. So, let's imagine our future as a time of being the wise elder and being of service to others; being a good example to those who will follow us of how life can be.

What if I never sort my life out?

When we are younger, we think that, in time, we will sort our life out, that everything will fall into place if we can solve one thing or another; that we will then reach our perfect life. However, as we age, we gain wisdom as we realise life will continue to have challenges, there will be more regrets, and we should accept that.

We may have felt that life would be better if we changed jobs, got a new relationship, lost 20 pounds, but what if all the stuff that's happening in our life, what if none of it is a mistake. It is the universe's plan to make us whole. We may never be fully happy in a relationship, our partner's habits continue to irritate us, or we may never maintain a new habit of 'eating clean', but that is not what life is about. All the steps we take to move to our goals, that is what life is about.

If we have never done before, now is the time we should be kind to ourselves; when we need to understand ourselves, and other people better, and to recognise that we don't always get things right; and the importance of forgiveness, especially of ourselves. It helps us to then role-model this to others.

My personal reflection

From working fairly full-time, I realised the nature of my work was no longer meaningful for me and through experiences and further learning, my life has segued to a more nature-based approach to working with individuals and to helping them find greater meaning, alongside a greater interest and usage of the depth of consciousness research by Carl Jung.

I can look back over my life to date and think of choices I could have made but accept that 'we are where we are' and that what seemed like a poor choice has led to better things.

I appreciate what I have now and look forward to ageing, recognising my health will decline but not to let that stop me to continue to have my best life. I now seek greater meaning in life and have flexible plans for the years ahead.

AUTHENTIC SELF

The search for our authentic self can lead to deep questions that may never have been considered; questions such as 'I have done the expected things, according to my best understanding of myself and the world, so why does my life not feel right?'[8] It may be that it is finding meaning in life that is the way to address this and this section focuses on this.

The Jungian psychologist James Hillman[9] has argued that the purpose of human ageing is to fulfil our true character, to become our essential selves. This is something philosophers have discussed across millennia; Epicurus said that happiness can best be achieved if we free ourselves from the prison of everyday business and politics. You can only do this with freedom from full-time work, and Epicurus and friends were happy to accept less money for independence. Sounds like a flexible approach with part-time working in retirement!

If we can't be who we are now, when can we ever? This is the time to be true to ourselves and to focus on a life well-lived. I want us to look back from our future self, when we are old-old and think that while life may not have gone easy, we had a fulfilled life.

WISDOM AND ELDERHOOD

We have such potential with ageing. Carl Jung succinctly said: "A human being would certainly not grow to be 70 or 80 years old if this longevity had no meaning for the species. The afternoon of human life must also have a significance of its own." Everyone gets older, but not all become an elder, and you can't just call yourself an elder; you need to prepare, transition, and be accepted by others. We also need to have forgiven ourselves, and others.

As people age, wisdom tends to grow, particularly among those who possess a high level of openness to new experiences, the ability to introspect and self-examine, a desire for personal growth, and a willingness to remain sceptical of their own perspectives. These individuals continually question their assumptions and beliefs, while exploring and evaluating new information that pertains to their sense of identity.[10] To what extent do you consider yourself an elder?

Activity 13.5

Chip Conley, co-founder of Modern Elder Academy[11] talks about being a modern elder. He created a list of ten statements[12] where you give yourself one point if it fully resonates, half if you are somewhat there, and zero if it doesn't resonate. Read these questions and give yourself a score.

---

1. Outside of my family, I am often in environments where I am the oldest or one of the oldest, and I don't hide my age.
2. I am both a lifelong learner and a 'long-life learner', someone who wants to live a life that's as deep and meaningful as it is long.
3. I enjoy growing older, and I believe my best work and life are ahead of me.
4. I feel like my ego is no longer my primary operating system, and I have a growing stirring in my soul.
5. I have developed an active practice of cultivating and harvesting wisdom based on metabolising my life experiences, and I can teach others to do the same.
6. I love becoming a new beginner at something and am endlessly curious.
7. I believe my emotional intelligence has grown, and I'm less reactive than I was ten years ago.
8. I have moved from the accumulation stage of my life to the editing stage. I am good at ending projects, relationships, mindsets, and distractions that don't feel nourishing or allow me to serve others effectively.

9. People tell me that I'm a great mentor and a conduit for wisdom. I would be honored to be called a 'wisdom worker' instead of a 'knowledge worker'.
10. I no longer define myself based on my achievements, image, status, or power, as I'm more focused on my purpose and legacy. The sentence 'I am what survives me' defines my life today.

Your score will be from 0 to 10. If you score below 5, you may like to look at the questions where you score 0 and think about action steps you could take to agree more with the statement.

LEGACY

Many people think legacy is meant for those who have a lot of money and are known as philanthropists. Or they are people such as Martin Luther King and Mother Teresa, activists and saints doing important work. But we can all leave a legacy.

Whilst we are likely to leave money to family and other bequests, we can leave a legacy through our behaviour and way of being. Legacy can be how we relate to other people, and can include small actions, such as showing other people how we live a life that is in line with our values and providing guidance to others. We can show others how we focus on the important things in life and how we can let go of failures. We can also do practical things such as writing our memoir or researching family history that we can pass on to others.

Being a mentor

Generativity often leads to people taking part in activity that will contribute to the community, both now and for future generations. This can include cross-generational activity such as mentoring younger people, coaching, or teaching. Mentorship is a relationship in which a more experienced or more knowledgeable person helps to guide a less experienced or less knowledgeable person, and the mentor can be older or younger. We covered mentoring briefly in Chapter 9. It can be formal, through work or in an organisation, or informal – a conversation with people you may have been introduced to through your church, interest group, or voluntary organisation, or by friends.

Some people will seek you out for your knowledge, especially in a work setting, or to support a new entrepreneur. Other relationships can focus on helping the mentee understand more about who they are and to help them to gain confidence. It could be with a university student, or a young person living alone for the first time. And we, too, may like to seek out a mentor, perhaps from a different generation, to learn new things such as using technology and social media.

AGEING

We are ageing from the day we are born. There is much written about successful ageing but success in later life is constructed in similar ways to success in younger years. It appears as a euphemism for not ageing at all; both the appearance and attributes of continued youthfulness are prized.[13] We covered views on ageing in chapter 3 and you answered questions on your views on ageing in Activity 3.11 in that chapter, on page 45, you may like to review your notes in your journal. Remember, a positive attitude can add over seven years to our lifetime.

Successful ageing is increasingly implicated in discussions about work in later life and creates a new distinction: those who achieve successful ageing through continued youthfulness versus those who do not.[14] Most people I talk with are more interested in staying healthy and being happy with how they look, much less about having cosmetic surgery to look young, but we all should be free to do whatever helps us feel more confident and happier.

We have our own thoughts and views on how we will age, and what we want to do, or not do. We now have more men dyeing their hair, and more women stopping and reclaiming their natural hair colour. Age is a state of mind. At 50, you can be old and stagnating or still growing at 100+. I often say to people that I don't fear death; what I fear is a life unlived. I see myself as evolving over time.

This is a topic we could discuss at length, and the subject matter for my next book on ageing, elderhood, and wisdom, but for now, I'd like to share two areas.

How old are you in your head?

Gerontology researchers will ask people "How old do you feel?", and most people who answer respond in physical terms, considering any ailments and the effect on them. A different question is "How old are you, in your head?" Danish research[15] has shown that, with adults over 40, on average people give an age of about 20 per cent younger than their chronological age.

What we find is that, when asked, someone of 76 immediately says 45. A woman of 53 says 36 and talks about her positive experiences of life at that time. A man of 53 says 35, as this was the age when he was happy with his life questions. We can also be frozen at an earlier life due to some unhappy or traumatic life experiences. This tends to be a Western phenomenon with a greater difference between chronological and subjective age with people from the United States, Western Europe, and Australia/Oceania and a lower difference in Africa.[16]

The age we say is our subjective age. This seems to link to optimism; rather than to deny our age, if we feel younger, we act younger, and don't let things stop us. Viewing ourselves as younger, and a belief that we are still useful and valuable, is a positive, and it doesn't need to rely on subjective age.

With a chronological age of 65, I could say my subjective age is 52; this was a time when I was successful in work, not overweight, and my relationship was positive. I am, however, very happy to tell people my age, to own my age, and to not let anything stop me doing, or being, what I can be. I still have long-term plans and have a positive vision of myself. There are a good number of people, me included, who are happy to be the age we are; we welcome the wisdom gained, the lessons learned.

We really are younger than in previous generations

Some interesting research compared people, aged 75 to 80 who were born 28 years apart.[17] They found that the second cohort had better physical functioning: walking 0.2 to 0.4 miles per second faster; a 5 to 25 per cent increase in grip-strength and knee-extension strength increased by 20 to 47 per cent. This is evidence that we are healthier for longer and we can reap these benefits if we stay physically active. There is also evidence that education helps us to live more healthier; we eat better and we know more about nutrition.

YOUR FUTURE SELF AT 90

Life is a journey to wholeness. Wholeness includes un-wholeness, which is where you can accept the imperfect, broken part of yourself, and also of everyone else. This is part of wisdom. We may wonder about what might have been, but this wonder is one of kind curiosity. What is most important is what is right for us now and will be right for us in the future. By paying more attention to our senses, especially our feelings, we are more likely to accept how things are and what comes next.

Activity 13.6

Earlier I asked you to consider your life looking two and five years ahead. Let's now take a longer view and imagine your life at 90, or 25 years into the future. I want you to write about your life then. Your relationships, health, how you have found meaning, your legacy. How are you? Take ten minutes to write whatever comes into your mind. As you sit there at 90, I then want you to look back over the past 20+ years. What are you most proud of? What stands out as part of your legacy?

AS WE END THIS BOOK

I have loved being on this journey with you. This is a wonderful time to reach this life stage and we are so lucky to be here; many people never reached it. If you have enjoyed journalling, you may like to continue.

I'm in a happy place with my life; even looking back five years I would never have imagined that I would choose to work less and to spend more time in nature. I will continue to research around ageing, wisdom, and elderhood and already have things in hand for my next book.

I write regular articles, published on LinkedIn and on my websites. Feel free to sign up. I have plans to give talks to a wider audience, too.

Wishing you a wonderful future.

Dr Denise Taylor
www.denisetaylor.co.uk

NOTES

1 Pevny. R. (2014). *Conscious Living, Conscious Aging: Embrace & Savor Your Next Chapter, Beyond Words.*
2 Schachter-Shalomi, Z., & Miller, R. (2014). *From Age-Ing to Sage-Ing: A Profound New Vision of Growing Older, Balance.*
3 August, R.A. (2011b). Women's retirement meanings: Context, changes, and organizational lessons. *Gender in Management*, 26(5), 351–366.
4 Steger, M.F. (2012). Experiencing meaning in life: Optimal functioning at the nexus of well-being, psychopathology, and spirituality. In P. T. P. Wong (Ed.), *The Human Quest for Meaning: Theories, Research, and Applications* (165–184). Routledge/Taylor & Francis Group.
5 Carrillo, A., Martínez-Sanchis, M., Etchemendy, E., Baños, R.M. (2019). May Qualitative analysis of the Best Possible Self intervention: Underlying mechanisms that influence its efficacy. *PLoS One*, 17, 14(5).
6 Freeman, M. (1993). *Rewriting the Self. History, Memory, Narrative.* Routledge, London.
7 Campbell, J. (1949). *The Hero with A Thousand Faces.* New World Library.
8 Hollis, J. (2006). *Finding Meaning in the Second Half of Life.* Gotham Books.
9 Hillman, J. (1999). *The Force of Character and the Lasting Life.* Random House.
10 Jeste, D.V., & Lee, E.E. (2019). The emerging empirical science of wisdom: Definition, measurement, neurobiology, longevity, and interventions. *Harvard Review of Psychiatry*, 27(3), 127–140.

11 www.modernelderacademy.com

12 https://wisdomwell.modernelderacademy.com/are-you-a-modern
-elder-a-quiz

13 Andrews, M. (2009). The narrative complexity of successful ageing. *International Journal of Sociology and Social Policy*, 29(1/2), 73–83.

14 Foweraker, B., & Cutcher, L. (2020). An ageless gift: Reciprocity and value creation by and for older workers. *Work, Employment and Society*, 34(4), 533–549.

15 https://link.springer.com/content/pdf/10.3758/BF03193996.pdf

16 Pinquart, M., & Wahl, H.-W. (2021). Subjective age from childhood to advanced old age: A meta-analysis. *Psychology and Aging*, 36(3), 394–406.

17 Koivunen, Kaisa, Sillanpää, Elina, Munukka, Matti, Portegijs, Erja, & Rantanen, Taina. (2021). Cohort differences in maximal physical performance: A comparison of 75- and 80-year-old men and women born 28 years apart. *The Journals of Gerontology: Series A*, 76(7), 1251–1259.

INDEX

Printed in Great Britain
by Amazon